THE REFERENCE SHELF (Continued)

Volume 24

Volume 23

Volume 22

Volume 20

Volume 19

Volume 18

THE REFERENCE SHELF

Vol. 30   No. 2

DS889
V4

THE NEW JAPAN

Edited by
ELIZABETH AND VICTOR A. VELEN

THE H. W. WILSON COMPANY
NEW YORK   1958

54842

MAY '58

PREFACE

Japan today is in a unique historic situation. In less than a decade she was reduced from a would-be world conqueror to her original "core," a group of small, scattered, and economically dependent islands. Her natural hinterland, the land mass of the Asian continent, has been separated from Japan proper, its traditional industrial arsenal.

The crux of many of Japan's political, economic, and psychological problems lies in the enormously rapid pace of her industrialization. Within a generation, after the restoration of power to the Emperor Meiji in 1868, she was transformed from an agricultural, feudal society into the world's third most important industrial and military power. The development of a modern industrial society in a still medieval, peasant land created an internal crisis. Japanese industry, producing at full capacity and speed without any real home market, was forced to expand abroad. This led to the concept of the "Greater Asia Co-Prosperity Sphere" and to forty years of conquest.

Japan's defeat dealt a severe blow at home to the myth of Japanese superiority. It also left a dangerous power vacuum. This the American occupation attempted to fill. Under General MacArthur the occupying authorities sought to remodel Japanese society through a series of far-reaching reforms. They also drew up a constitution, later adopted by the Japanese, designed to establish the country on a new base—that of a Western-type parliamentary government.

Now, five years after the end of the occupation, the question remains as to whether this new democratic society is firmly rooted. In recent years both internal and external factors have intervened to hamper or to reverse the trend toward democratization in Japan; they also tend to pull her away from the West. To a certain extent political and economic power has returned almost automatically to those groups and interests which were wielding it in prewar Japan. The cold war has led to a reversal of American policy toward rearming Japan; a paradoxical situation has thereby arisen in that powerful forces in Japan now oppose rearmament and a military alliance with the West in the very name of the policies and aims of the American occupation. The Communist victory in China (1950) and the appearance of newly independent states among the formerly colonial territories in Asia have placed Japan in a new strategic relationship to Asia. Finally, Japan has been offered the bait of renewed leadership in Asia by the emergence of the "Bandung powers"—the anticolonial nations of the Asian-African Conference held at Bandung, Indonesia, in 1955.

These pressures combined may account for the increasingly neutral role Japan has adopted in world affairs, notably in the United Nations.

The purpose of this book is to give the background for an understanding of Japan today—of the complex and conflicting forces at work in the country. Some of the articles included are straight reporting of events; others represent the opinions of qualified observers. All were selected with an eye to giving the most relevant facts as well as a balanced picture.

The editors wish to thank the various authors and publishers who have given their permission for the use of materials included in this book. They would like to express appreciation to Mr. Alan D. Smith of the Japanese Consulate General in New York for supplying material not readily available otherwise.

ELIZABETH AND VICTOR A. VELEN

January 1958

CONTENTS

I. LAND AND PEOPLE

EDITORS' INTRODUCTION

Our knowledge of the Japanese has increased immeasurably as a result of the American occupation. To the American soldier stationed in Japan the Japanese were surprisingly unlike the picture of them painted by the wartime press. Far from resembling a nation of tough military extremists dominated by a fanatical emperor, the country appeared to be populated by gentle, cultivated tea drinkers and colorful geisha girls. A look beneath the surface, however, would have revealed the Japanese as they really are—a proud and insular people steeped in the traditions of an ancient, Asian culture.

Japanese life today is a curious mixture of age-old ritual and modern innovations adopted from the West, particularly from the United States. An understanding of this dual character of postwar Japanese society is essential to a grasp of the country's present problems.

In this section an attempt is made to show modern Japan in brief perspective—its land and people, its history, its religion, its cultural history, and its popular arts. These are dealt with in five background articles. The concluding article gives a rounded impression of modern Japanese life.

JAPAN AS IT IS TODAY [1]

Territory

An insular country situated off the eastern edge of the Asian continent, Japan is composed of the four main

[1] From pamphlet published by the Public Information and Cultural Affairs Bureau, Japanese Ministry of Foreign Affairs. Tokyo. 1956. (Obtainable from Information Office, Consulate General of Japan, 3 East 54th Street, New York 22) p5-10. Reprinted by permission.

islands of Hokkaido, Honshu, Shikoku and Kyushu and some thousand smaller islands and islets which lie adjacent to them.

Japan lost 45.5 per cent of its prewar territory as a result of the war and is now a country of only 141,529 square miles. A comparison with other countries shows that it is one eighth the size of India, less than one twentieth the size of the United States, one fifty-eighth the size of U.S.S.R. or 1.5 times as large as the size of the United Kingdom.

Small though it is, Japan has a wealth of scenic beauty. Situated in the temperate zone, the entire land is robed in verdure. With high volcanic mountains, lakes brimming with limpid waters, rivers dashing through craggy gorges and stripes of neatly cultivated paddies and fields, the whole of Japan gives the appearance of a beautiful natural park.

Topography

Japan is a mountainous country. Mountains with peaks higher than 2,000 meters (6,561.68 feet) above sea level number 250. The highest and most famed is majestic Mt. Fuji which towers 3,773 meters (12,378.6 feet) above sea level.

Being of volcanic origin, the Japanese islands abound with volcanoes—both dormant and active. Of the 192 volcanoes located in Japan, 58 are active.

Extensive plains are few in Japan, but the ones that do exist are of great economic importance to the population and provide much of its food supply.

Japan is surrounded by water. Its coast line is 17,150 miles long (about twice that of the United States). The shores of the Sea of Japan are comparatively regular,

but those facing the Pacific Ocean are indented with a
large number of gulfs, bays and inlets, many of which
offer excellent anchorages. Harbors are thus numerous;
some of them, including the two principal ones—Yokohama and Kobe—are kept busy with ocean-going vessels.

Climate

Japan is noted for its mild and temperate climate,
and . . . since it is surrounded by sea, Japan's climate
is considerably influenced by two ocean currents which
flow around Japan. They are "Kuroshio" and
"Oyashio." "Kuroshio," meaning black current, originates north of the Philippines and flows along the eastern
coast of the main island and "Oyashio" originates in the
Arctic and washes the shore of the northern part of the
main island, meeting the Kuroshio. The first is warm
and the second cold.

Generally speaking, four seasons of the year follow
one another with a clear-cut regularity in Japan. On no
occasion does winter telescope into spring with late
snow, or summer blaze loiter into autumn. . . .

Rainfall is heavy, ranging from 40 to 100 inches
annually and snowfall is frequent and heavy in northern
Japan.

Population

With more than 89 million people living within its
limited territory, Japan has the fifth largest population
in the world. Only China, India, the Soviet Union and
the United States outrank Japan in this respect.

In contrast to these nations, however, all of which
are huge in area, Japan is very small. The total Japanese land area is . . . about the size of the state of Mon-
tana in the United States. Japan thus has a population
density of about 630 persons per square mile.

Belgium and the Netherlands have a higher rate of population density than Japan. When, however, computed on the basis of per square mile of arable land, Japan is without comparison. Only about 15 per cent of Japan's total land area is arable, which means that more than 4,200 persons live in one square mile of cultivated land, a much higher rate than that of any other nation in the world.

Figures compiled in 1780 and 1846 indicate that the Japanese population remained comparatively stable at about 26 million for more than a century preceding the Meiji Restoration in 1868. The natural increase in population which multiplied the Japanese population by more than three times and brought it to the 89 million mark is, therefore, a phenomenon of the past ninety years. In Japan, as in the case of European nations, an increase in population followed the advent of modern industry.

The increase in population was not so spectacular during the war, as shown by the fact that the population of Japan was approximately 71.4 million (excluding the population in Korea, Formosa and Sakhalin) in 1940 and 72.2 million in 1945.

In the postwar years, however, Japan's population rose sharply to 83.2 million in 1950 and reached 89.3 million in 1955. In other words, the increase during the first half period (1945-1950) was 11.2 million and during the latter (1950-1955) was 6.1 million. . . .

It is estimated, on the basis of the current rates of births and deaths, that Japan will have a population of 100 million within fifteen years.

A CHRONOLOGY OF JAPANESE HISTORY [2]

Legends and archaeological remains suggest that disparate races were fused in prehistoric times. The first emperor, Jimmu, came to the throne about 660 B.C.

c.400: Introduction of Chinese learning to Japan.

552: Buddhism imported from Korea. Clan warfare.

645: Overthrow of the Soga clan by the first of the Fujiwara, a family which virtually ruled Japan for centuries by controlling the hereditary line of emperors.

710-784: The Nara period. First permanent capital at Nara. Compilation of legendary histories such as the *Kojiki* and *Nihonshoki*. Flowering of literature, including the *Manyoshu* poetry collection. Buddhist sculpture and rise of painting.

794-1185: The Heian Period. Capital moved to Kyoto. Art and literature flourished. The *Tale of Genji* written by Lady Murasaki about 1000. Struggles among feudal clans, later immortalized in Noh and Kabuki plays.

1185-1333: The Kamakura Period. Continuing struggles for power among rival feudal lords and their knights. Emperors dominated by these Shoguns (generalissimos). Invading Mongol Armada, sent by Kubla Khan, destroyed by typhoon in 1281.

1333-1568: The Muromachi Period. Ashikaga family Shoguns in power at Kyoto and great art patrons. Monochrome ink-wash in painting. Noh dramas. Constant civil wars. Trade with the West opened by Portuguese in 1542. St. Francis Xavier brought Christianity in 1549.

[2] Reprinted from *Atlantic Monthly*. 195:174. January 1955. Courtesy of "Perspective of Japan," published by Intercultural Publications Inc. Reprinted by permission of Intercultural Publications Inc.

1582-1600: The Momoyama Period. Hideyoshi unified Japan, then tried to annex Korea. Kyoto destroyed in civil wars and rebuilt. A new, florid style in art.

1600-1867: The Edo Period. Tokugawa family Shoguns with capital at Edo (now Tokyo). Outlying regions ruled by feudal Daimyo lords. Samurai warriors became a fixed aristocracy. Commerce with Western traders until all but Dutch expelled in 1640. Rising merchant class held down politically. Christianity suppressed; Confucianism encouraged. Another great age of literature and art. Kabuki drama flourishing. Ukiyo-e wood-block print books. Hiroshige and Hokusai, great artists.

1853: Commodore Perry's visit; reopening of trade.

1868-1912: The Meiji Period. Emperors take back control from Shoguns and power from Daimyos and undertake modernization of Japan along Western lines. Emphasis on education. Extensive social reforms culminating in Meiji Constitution and first Diet in 1890. Sino-Japanese War in 1894-1895. Russo-Japanese War in 1904-1905. Korea annexed in 1910. Building up of navy.

1912-1926: The Taisho Period. A liberal era with party governments in power. "Proletarian movement" in literature. Despite strong German influence in Meiji Period, Japan sided with the Allies in First World War. Earthquake destroyed Tokyo in 1923.

1926-1940: Liberal elements outmaneuvered by those favoring imperialist expansion into Asia. Japan moved into Manchuria in 1931 and war with China began in 1937. Orderly party government gave way to virtual military dictatorships. Japanese troops entered Indo-China and alliance with Germany and Italy in 1940.

1941-1945: World War II. Japanese overran most of Southeast Asia, but were finally defeated.

1945-1952: Allied occupation of Japan. Attempt to "democratize" Japan largely successful. Restoration of party government and suppression of militarism. Economic recovery. Korean War began in 1950.

RELIGION [3]

The following three major religions exist in Japan: Shintoism, Buddhism and Christianity.

Shintoism is Japan's indigenous cult. The Imperial as well as the family ancestors are worshipped and it is not a religion in a strict sense. It was, however, regarded as a state religion during World War II when it was encouraged by the government. After the cessation of the war, it became an ordinary religion. Two universities are operated by the Shinto organization.

Buddhism was introduced to Japan from India through China and Korea, around the middle of the sixth century. While it greatly contributed to the promotion of learning and the arts, Buddhism also flourished as a religion. Twelve universities are operated by Buddhist organizations. The number of people who belonged to its numerous sects or subsects were approximately 45.4 million in 1943 and 47.7 million in 1953.

Christianity was introduced to Japan by St. Francis Xavier, a Jesuit Father, in 1549. Although it prospered rapidly at first with the encouragement of Shoguns during the latter half of the sixteenth century, Christianity came under prohibition during the course of 250 years that followed until the middle of the nineteenth century, when Japan opened its doors to foreign nations. . . . Christian organizations now operate twenty-two univer-

[3] From "Japan as It Is Today," pamphlet published by the Public Information and Cultural Affairs Bureau, Japanese Ministry of Foreign Affairs. Tokyo. 1956. p85. Reprinted by permission.

sities. There were approximately 277,000 Christians in 1943 and 485,000 in 1953. Protestants outnumber the Catholics slightly.

Besides these three major religions, there are many other religious organizations. Some of them have expanded considerably in postwar years.

Confucianism is regarded by some as a religion. It is, however, a code of moral precepts rather than a religion. It was introduced to Japan at the beginning of the sixth century and exerted a tremendous influence on the minds of Japanese people . . . until the end of the recent war. It has declined, however, relatively in the postwar period.

JAPAN'S CULTURAL HISTORY [4]

The progress of history has so accelerated that a century now witnesses the profound changes that once took several centuries. This is especially true of the Orient, which until recently stood apart from the central movements of world culture. Japan is the most remote of the Oriental nations and was the last to be washed by the tide of Western culture. But the changes that occurred throughout the Orient after its meeting with the West took place more swiftly in Japan than in any of her neighbors. Japan had to rush along the road which the West had followed at a more leisurely pace since the Renaissance, and in that cultural race Japan proved herself swift-footed. I refer, of course, to Japan since the Meiji Restoration of 1868. . . .

The modern Japanese is sometimes criticized for forgetting history. The Japanese of the early Meiji Period,

[4] From "Japan's 'Cultural Democracy'" by Nyozekan Hasegawa, Japanese journalist and novelist. Translated by William Candlewood. *Atlantic Monthly.* 195:170-3. January 1955. Courtesy of "Perspective of Japan," published by Intercultural Publications Inc. Reprinted by permission of Intercultural Publications Inc.

when I was born, was moving forward with the vigor necessary to jump from the old feudal state to the modern state, but at the same time past history was with him, not simply as a memory, but as a concrete part of his life. The "child of Meiji," as he is called in Japan, therefore had in himself, as his period had in itself, a progressive side and a conservative side. In that I think he was a little like the modern Englishman. Actually, this conflict has been true of every period in Japanese history.

The Japanese nature contains many varied elements. Native Shinto is the racial religion, and yet long ago Buddhism was accepted from the continent and peacefully amalgamated with Shinto. The two faiths, native and imported, have lived side by side. St. Francis Xavier, who came to Japan in the sixteenth century, reported in his letters that in the same family parents and children or brothers and sisters might belong to different sects.

This is true not only of religion but of culture in general. The Japanese, individually and socially, has a malleability which makes it possible for him to incorporate these varied elements. The persecution of Christians toward the end of the Middle Ages is a blot quite without parallel in earlier Japanese history, but it is rather different from the intolerance of medieval Europe. The Dutch, who were in a position of particular intimacy with the Japanese, passed on information on the record of aggression by European powers in the Far East, and it was the fear that Christian missionaries were the spearhead of colonialism that led to the persecution.

After that, Japan sealed herself from the world except for some commercial relations with the Dutch from whom the Japanese learned something of contemporary Europe. Inside Japan a flowering called by historians the "Japanese Renaissance" took place in the seventeenth century. This awakening, fostered by the stable government of our Edo Period, may be compared to the European stage of development from warring feudal states to free guild cities. I would like to suggest that our Renaissance was possible because certain "modern" characteristics were already to be found in Japan at the dawn of history.

In a sense, Japan has always been a "national" state. With no interruption it has been a nation of one people through more than two thousand years. Not one among the empires of Europe and Asia escaped internal territorial and racial conflicts, but Japan did. As anthropologists point out, the Japanese nation is compounded of various strains, but even as early as the "period of the gods," a single Yamato people had developed a belief in a common ancestry. Earlier there had been two dominant peoples, the Yamato and the Izumo, who set up rival states, but the Yamato absorbed the Izumo, and the legendary ancestors of both were united in the great shrines of Ise and Izumo, where they are still worshiped today. . . .

The Japanese, held together by belief in a common ancestry, were never conquered by another people. And Japan lost her sphere of influence in Korea in ancient times, so that "imperialism" had no chance to show itself until our day, either as imposed from abroad or as launched by the Japanese themselves. Japan resembled, politically and socially, an advanced development of the primitive clan-state.

Immigrants from abroad comprised no small part of the population in prehistoric and early historic times, but without exception they were swiftly assimilated, and though legally they were registered as "foreign clans," they were, except for distinguishing physical characteristics, no different from the Yamato people. This great power of assimilation is to be explained by the fact that, as the population is made up of many elements, so also are cultural forms multiple, and it may be said that a "human" or active element prevails over a "racial" or passive element in the Japanese. And this, too, is one of the characteristics of the modern national state.

As a result of unification, Japan already had in the eighth century a national language such as reached maturity in Europe only with the modern age. A people's literature had arisen by the tenth century, and in the eleventh large numbers of novels and essays were written, including our greatest masterpiece the *Tale of Genji*.

The court early encouraged the spread of the Yamato language, and, to stimulate their composition, systematically collected poems and folk songs throughout the country, had them set to music, and included them in anthologies. The *Manyoshu,* a collection of some five thousand poems compiled over a long period by a number of editors, reflects the poetic concepts of the age, expressed in the Yamato language, from emperors, nobility, and warriors, down to the common people. Contemporary critics still give the *Manyoshu* the highest critical rating as poetry, not only because the language is so beautiful but also because the poetic emotions expressed have affinities with modern realism and romanticism—further evidence that the Japanese in ancient times had modern characteristics.

Modernism in Early Literature

This modernism of the ancient Japanese was inherent in our culture in the period covered by the legends of

the gods. One of the prime scriptures of our Shinto
religion, the *Kojiki* ("Records of Ancient Matters"),
compiled in 712, represents Japanese literature in its
most primitive form. The first half of the *Kojiki* deals
with the gods, but these gods do not have the heroic
qualities of those in the legends of other countries.
They are described as thoroughly human. They participate only in the production of the things of nature, and
even here they have not the power to make rivers and
mountains, but only to create the staples of an agrarian
society—and these almost as if by accident, one product
rising quite by chance from another.

The legends of our gods are in the naturalist-realist
vein that has characterized so much of Japanese literature. The one heroic god in the pantheon, Susanoo-no-
mikoto, was purged for his violence. Japan, we are told,
was founded by the Sun Goddess—a survival of sun
worship—but she was feminine in nature, and she fled
from Susanoo's violence into a cave, leaving the world
in darkness, subsequently to be lured out again by an
amusing dance performed by another goddess. It is
notable that our legends frequently recount similar vic-
tories of the weak over the strong.

The latter half of the *Kojiki* treats of the earliest
historical period, and, as the scholar Norinaga has
pointed out, it is a matter-of-fact history in no way
distorted by ideology. Its rationale is not far from that
of modern historiography—and this already in the eighth
century.

And even in those days, thanks to the unified Yamato
language, there was a form of education such that literature and history spread through the land like folklore.
Villagers in the remotest countryside sang Yamato
songs. History was transmitted through *kataribe*, "reci-

ters," and as Japan had no native system of writing, Chinese characters were used phonetically by the upper classes to take down the history thus recited. This verbal tradition was preserved particularly well in aristocratic houses and provided material for the *Kojiki* and the *Nihonshoki,* another collection of legends. . . .

The Japanese character reveals itself most clearly in literature. In my opinion the history of Japanese literature shows less evolution in tendency than that of Europe, which moved from classicism through romanticism to realism and naturalism, while in our literature, from the tenth century onward, the realistic and naturalistic strains have been dominant over the classical and the romantic. I attribute this largely to the fact that Chinese characters were not long retained as our chief written language, giving way to a simple phonetic system which adequately represents the fifty syllables of our spoken language. The first condition for the rise of realistic literature is a system of writing which reproduces colloquial speech.

From the tenth century on Japanese could be noted down with rigid formality in the fifty phonetic signs. These were later reduced to forty-eight, and, like the alphabet, the series was named for its first letters (in this case, the three sounds *i, ro, ha*). Anyone who knew these forty-eight symbols could read all the literature of the day. Until the end of the Edo Period (1600-1867), works completely in the phonetic syllabary were common, and the highest literary achievement thus reached down to the lowest strata of society.

In the Middle Ages it became the custom for even pure Japanese to be translated into Chinese, and this affected speech, so that the Japanese sentence became a mixture of pure Japanese (in the phonetic script) and

Chinese. Few, however, except the nobility, the warrior class, and scholars, had an opportunity to study Chinese and in due course the Chinese characters used in writing also came to be transcribed after their sounds into the phonetic script so that they could be read by the populace at large. As a result the demand for historical and literary works increased, and to satisfy it—there was no printing in those days and hand-copied texts were costly —the art of reciting grew rapidly from around the fourteenth century. Blind priests made their living by singing historical narratives in the streets to the simple accompaniment of a sort of mandolin. The classic Noh drama which survives today is a product of the same epoch. Its content was influenced by a sort of Buddhist romanticism, for by the fourteenth century Buddhism had spread from the upper classes to the masses. Yet this romanticism in Noh was balanced by the realism of Kyogen, the comic interludes . . . interspersed with the serious plays. The vein of Kyogen resembles the realism of Molière, though Kyogen predated Molère by three centuries.

"Cultural Democracy"

In the Edo Period, literature and the arts flourished in Edo (the present Tokyo) and Osaka as never before in Japanese history. Unlike the West, however, where the old was usually discarded for the new, in Japan the historical and the contemporary existed side by side. All periods in Japanese history were piled one on another to give form to the Edo Period.

On top, so to speak, of the old Noh drama the Bunraku puppet theatre and the Kabuki theatre developed. Noh continued to be performed, in theory only for the Samurai—it was forbidden to the commoner—but actually it was widely appreciated, the prohibition being little more than a form. [In Noh, the oldest form of Japanese drama, the action is a form of stately dance with strict, conventional gestures; narrative choruses and orchestral music provide accompaniment. In Kabuki, the most popular form of drama, the action combines singing, dancing, and pantomime; the acting is stylized, but less restrained than in Noh. Both Noh and Kabuki have repertoires of poetic plays using historical and legendary material, and in both feminine roles are taken by men.— Eds.] In prose, the fantasies of the Muromachi Period gave way to more modern romances and novels. Critics have noted that Edo literature was rather similar to English literature during and after the Renaissance. The playwright Chikamatsu is often compared to Shakespeare, the romancer Bakin to Scott, and Edo humor to that of Dickens and Thackeray.

The art of wood-block printing saw marked advances in the Edo Period, and a wide variety of literature was transcribed into the phonetic syllabary and published with Ukiyo-e-style illustrations as *ezoshi*, "picture books," a popular form that reached to every level of society. Romances were imported from China and translated in large numbers. Even in an age that did not know movable type, books printed from wood blocks were published in very large editions. By the Edo Period the illiteracy rate was extremely low, and even the illiterate could become familiar with the contents of literary and historical works by hearing them read or recited. Thus the finest works of literature became accessible to the lowest levels of society. Japan was politically a most undemocratic country, but culturally it was from its beginnings one of the most democratic societies. I like to call this Japan's "cultural democracy."

When I was asked once by an American professor what I meant by my term "cultural democracy," I cited the Katsura Imperial Villa near Kyoto, which is . . . [an excellent illustration].. I pointed out that it is an extremely small and simple wooden building, somewhat different in its form from the house of a commoner but no different in its basic principles. It does not suggest wealth and power as do European palaces. It has none of their decorations and elaborations; it is simplicity itself. Smaller in scale than even the houses of the wealthy and noble, it is a symbol of the way in which the Imperial Family held itself aloof from politics, rather as in a modern democracy. Like the English monarch today, our Emperor reigned but did not rule.

To be sure, the Emperor was deified, but, he was a most human god, a model of humanism, quite divorced from military power, which was in the hands of the Shoguns and, in our time, of the generals and their clique. The shrines where the Imperial ancestors are worshiped are termed "great" shrines, but they are actually even smaller than the Villa, and Ise, the greatest shrine of all, is a simple little building not as large as the house of a small landowner. Anyone familiar with the grandeur of St. Peter's in Rome is no doubt surprised when he sees the modesty of the building in which is enshrined the ancestor of the Japanese race. This I consider a typical manifestation of Japanese "cultural democracy."

The finest art and literature of the Edo Period was popular. The Ukiyo-e print, now recognized throughout the world as the highest product of wood-block art, was provided in every household for the education of children, and in middle-class families prints were collected year by year for generations, so that the family collection was larger than that of the specialized collector today. A wood-block portrait by Sharaku that would now sell for tens of thousands of yen, was one of my childhood companions, along with my picture book. As a child I enjoyed too the series of Ukiyo-e prints called the "Genji-e," a widely read modernized version of the *Tale of Genji*. A further example of the democratic vein in our literature is Saikaku Ibara's tale in this collection, the story of the niece of a proud feudal Daimyo who dared to accept the love of a commoner.

As with literature, so with the theatre, where art of the highest order was appreciated by the lower levels of society. Square, straw-matted stalls were provided at the Kabuki-Za so that the whole family could see the play together, and I can remember how as children we went with our parents to the theatre. The most demanding critics of the Kabuki were from the Tokyo artisan and working class. It was the custom to shout words of criticism or approval at the stage, and the most enthusiastic always came from the highest and cheapest balconies. The man in the street was skilled at mimicking the speeches and motions of the great actors such as Danjuro and Kikugoro. When I was in London some fifty years ago, I asked if workers could imitate Tree and Irving, the great English actors of the day. I was told that such a thing would be impossible in Europe or America. But it was possible in Japan as late as my childhood. . . .

Western Influence

The characteristics of Japanese culture which I have stressed persisted into the late nineteenth century, but from the beginning of the Taisho Period (1912 to 1926) far-reaching social and cultural changes began to set in.

European influence took hold and the highest culture soon became the property of the intelligentsia and the economically privileged classes. The masses were left at a distance from it, with a lower-level literature and art of their own. Not only were the best things the most expensive and thus beyond the reach of the masses, but their Westernized content was beyond popular comprehension. This sudden intrusion of alien forces led to a distorted sort of culture in which a form reached high quality only when it was divorced from the masses. "Cultural democracy" declined.

What was the nature of the Western tide that swept over Japan? In the early Meiji Period Japan had pursued Anglo-Saxon culture, attracted by its liberal spirit. But from the mid-Meiji Period, leaders in the bureaucracy, the armed forces, and the academic world began to feel that Japan's position in the Far East was not unlike that of Germany in Europe. They therefore proceeded to replace their Anglo-American model with a German one. Misguided by the currents of the time, they tried to make their debut on the stage of twentieth century history in German costume and make-up, adopting a transcendentalism and idealism diametrically opposed to our traditional realism and naturalism. Japanese civilization became highly Germanized, and the country was finally led to the same fate as the German Empire.

Since her defeat Japan has been forced to devote her whole effort toward reorganizing the nation in the direction of modern history. The most fortunate factor in this situation is the tradition of "cultural democracy" which Japan possessed from its origins down to the Meiji Period. I find our oldest traditions are in accord with the most advanced steps forward.

Nevertheless I am disturbed by doubts as to whether most Japanese, not yet free from the influence of the un-Japanese elements of education in the Taisho Period and after, are yet properly conscious of their own true national character. The ruling class in particular seems to lack this consciousness. Yet it is hard to believe that the traditional traits in a national history of over two thousand years can be destroyed by the distortions of less than half a century. Provided the Japanese do not give up the desire to return to their own fundamental nature, the day when they will do so cannot be far away.

THE POPULAR ARTS IN JAPAN [5]

Motion Pictures

Of the five hundred films shown yearly in Japan, half are Japanese and the remainder mainly American, followed by French. Immediately after the war, Japanese audiences showed little interest in native products, but in 1953 the trend was reversed and box-office receipts from Japanese films now far exceed those from foreign ones. This change can be attributed to the growing skill of Japanese directors, the foreign awards which their films have received, and the reawakening of patriotic sentiment among the people.

This new trend began with the spectacular success abroad of *Rashomon,* directed by Akira Kurosawa, and virtually ignored in Japan until it won the film awards of Venice and of the American Academy. Based on a story by Ryunosuke Akutagawa, in which an outlaw

[5] From "Popular Entertainments of Japan," by Koji Ozaki, drama critic. Translated by Donald Keene. *Atlantic Monthly.* 195:148-51. January 1955. Courtesy of "Perspective of Japan," published by Intercultural Publications Inc. Reprinted by permission of Intercultural Publications Inc.

violates a woman before her husband's eyes, the film posed the question: was the woman attracted by the savagery of the man, or did she yield to save her husband?

Another Venice prize winer, *Ugetsu,* directed by Kenji Mizoguchi, tells of an ambitious potter, so eager for wealth that he leaves his wife in the ravaged countryside to sell his wares in the city. There, a beautiful woman orders him to her home. He succumbs to her beauty only to discover that she is a ghost, the last daughter of a ruined clan, and that association with her will be fatal. Awakening from the spell, he hastens home only to find that his wife has been killed. Both direction and photography reflect the story's blending of realism and fantasy, most notably in the subtle interweaving of time present and time past.

The Tale of Genji, based on the eleventh century classic novel of Japanese court life, was directed by Kozaburo Yoshimura and won a Cannes award. A Venice award was given to *A Woman's Life,* also directed by Mizoguchi, and based on a novel by the seventeenth century author Saikaku Ibara.

Gate of Hell, superbly photographed in color and directed by Teinosuke Kinugasa, is placed in the feudal Heian Era. It is a tragic drama of unrequited passion and of a wife who sacrifices her life for her husband's honor. This film, too, won a prize at Cannes. Of all the Japanese films receiving foreign acclaim, only one, *The Place Where the Chimneys Are Seen,* had a modern theme. Directed by Heinosuke Gosho, it won an award in Berlin.

Despite the many real advances made by Japanese films, there are recurrent themes and situations which reflect the old-fashioned and feudal elements still surviving in social custom. For example: once a woman is married she must never, for any reason, leave her husband's house and must comply with his will. If a family is extremely poor, they may sell their daughter, and the girl does not hesitate to sacrifice herself to provide for her parents. Such things do still take place, occasionally, in present-day Japan and there are films which exploit these ideas and include all the other trappings and symbols of old Japan — the master-retainer relationships (which always accompany sword fighting), clan feuds, and anachronistic dramatic situations. Certainly such themes do appeal to the Japanese. Tragedies, acted in a style half-classical and half-realistic, usually center on fatalistic sacrifices. The Japanese, who weep at these films, respond more to the emotions depicted than to the plot itself.

Along with these ancient themes is a fairly heavy emphasis on tragic love. We still do not have the habit of kissing in public, but the films are breaking down this restriction. Before the war, kissing scenes in foreign films were generally deleted by order of the government. At first depicted with typical Japanese modesty—in the shade of a tree or behind a fan—the intense emotion of parting lovers has recently been shown a little more frankly, often by a kiss in the rain.

There is an effort among some of the younger directors to come to grips realistically with the misery of war and to portray the complicated ways in which modern people live—their struggles, their compromises, and their defeats. Such directors are incorporating new artistic elements into their work, and many now cooperate with authors in an attempt to criticize contemporary society.

Another interesting addition to film art has been provided by some of the older directors, and this is a re-creation of the emotion that one finds in such traditional arts as the Noh drama and Kabuki. They attempt, as far as possible, to stylize actuality, even in the dramatization of present-day events.

The making of Japanese films is primarily the responsibility of five major film companies, of which the largest, Shochiku, has a capital of the equivalent of $5 million and employs eighteen directors. Compared with foreign production, Japanese companies work at enormous speed. Each produces, for example, at least four films a month, and a director needs only ten days for a feature film.

Until very recently these five companies held a complete monopoly of the Japanese film world, and protected themselves by permanently barring an actor from employment by any of the major companies if he made a film outside their auspices. In 1930, in an attempt to break this monopoly, several small independent producers made films designed to combine entertainment with a social message of some sort. This effort, however, was short-lived. The major companies as a rule steered clear both of politics and of social problems.

Recently, the Nikkatsu Company also tried to challenge the supremacy of the Big Five. As yet, it cannot boast of any stars or first-rate directors, but its influence in the film world has been considerable and has revived the interest in independent producing companies. In fact, many stars now attempt to maintain a free status, and insist that their contracts include a clause allowing them to perform occasionally for other companies.

This trend has been further spurred as a result of the Red purge carried out in the big companies. Many excellent technicians of Leftist politics have now begun to make films independently or with the help and cooperation of labor unions. One of Japan's more successful directors, Tadashi Imai, who used to work for one of the big companies, now devotes his time exclusively to independent productions. He created a sensation with his *School of Echoes,* which inquires into the problems of education in elementary schools, and his *Tower of Lilies,* which was based on the true story of the annihilation of girl students who served as nurses during the fighting on Okinawa—a film meant to highlight the tragedies of the war and the recklessness of the Japanese military. Independent producers concentrate on the production of antiwar films, for the major companies have so far shown no interest in such subjects. The Leftists, of course, openly use such themes for propaganda.

Television

Television in Japan is still on a fairly primitive level because neither of the two television networks, the government subsidized NHK, or the commercial NTV, has adequate facilities. A shortage of studios exists, and technical processes are still to be perfected. Yet a foreigner visiting a Japanese studio would, I think, be surprised at the ingenuity of the sets. The various properties are handmade and, for economy's sake, the producers have resorted to the ancient techniques of Japanese-style painting in the making of scenery. For instance, the feeling of dark or light colors is conveyed by the use only of black, white and grays.

The spread of television has been slow. There are at present about 30,000 receivers in operation, and both networks broadcast only five hours a day. When television broadcasts began, certain critics cynically remarked that it was a typically bad habit of the Japanese to start something before they were fully prepared for it. However, the potential popularity of television is now clearly evident. In Tokyo crowds of people gather before the shop windows which display television sets.

By far the most popular television programs are news, baseball, Japanese wrestling, boxing, and of course "pro-wrestling" or Western-style wrestling. Television drama is still in an embryonic state, and only three or four authors are writing what may properly be called television dramas, the most popular of which are comedies. About the only other type of play on television is the "home drama" which is directed at the entire family, and stresses common domestic problems. . . .

Even though original works written for television are still scarce and poor, the medium does serve to bring stage performances to a wider public. Telecasts of Kabuki performances, for instance, have been about the most popular dramatic shows to be put on. Stage performances of other kinds of theatre have also enjoyed considerable success. Now that an agreement has been reached with the film companies allowing the use of films that are at least three years old, television's prospects seem brighter.

Dancing

Before the war, there were in Japan only two schools of dancing—the traditional Japanese dance, and the modern dance imported from Europe. Since the war, ballet has been introduced, and has had such an immediate and widespread success that advertisements for "ballet academies" are now seen not only in Tokyo, but in the suburbs. This is one of the most inexplicable entertainment phenomena, for nothing could be farther in mood or technique from the classical dance of Japan.

The Japanese style of dancing has been for some time now controlled by four major schools. In order to become a dancer, a pupil must enter one of these schools and study with an approved teacher. When that teacher decides that the young dancer is sufficiently accomplished, the head of the school gives his consent for the dancer to appear in public and to use the school's name. Without this cachet, a dancer cannot perform as an independent artist.

This may appear excessively old-fashioned, but it is precisely because of this system that the Japanese classic dances have been preserved intact. However, it must be added that while this conservative system protects the classics and refines techniques, it seriously hinders the production of new works on modern themes.

Apart from the young girls of good families who study dancing as a pretty, drawing-room accomplishment, the chief exponents of traditional dancing are the geishas. To the Japanese, the word "geisha" has many beautiful associations, even though they know that poverty may have obliged a girl to take up the profession. For a Japanese audience, the brilliant spectacle of geisha dancing on the stage is one of the most moving and glamorous entertainments. In Tokyo, for instance, the Azuma Dance, an annual all-geisha performance, is one of the season's brightest events, as are the Miyako Dance and the Kamo River Dance in Kyoto.

In 1917, the geisha, Shizue Fujikage, who was at the time considered one of the foremost dancers, began to perform independently as an advocate of the "new" dance. She put together a repertory of dances based on modern themes, but performed with the traditional techniques. Most of the works of the traditional Japanese dance describe unhappy love affairs and Fujikage brought a welcome new note of gaiety, which has been carried on by her followers.

But recently, ballet has far surpassed in popularity the "new" dance, although there are, so far, only two full-size, professional ballet companies, and as yet no Japanese choreographer and no original Japanese ballets. The companies rely entirely on such perennial favorites as *Swan Lake, The Nutcracker Suite, Scheherazade,* and *Coppelia.*

Only one recent event has encouraged traditional Japanese dancers to feel that there is an active future for their art. This was the triumph of Tokuho Azuma in America. And although there were sharp protests because she styled herself "a Kabuki dancer," her success has given added confidence to classical dancers here in the face of trends that seem to draw more and more on the West.

Music

Just as ballet has come into its own in Japan's world of dance, so in music, opera is now claiming the greatest attention. Before the war, virtually the only Western vocal music heard in Japan were the German lieder, because the teachers in Japanese music schools were almost all Germans. Since the Occupation, however, the American fondness for *Madame Butterfly, The Mikado,* and the like, has stimulated Japanese musicians to explore the opera form, using native material.

There are said to be over thirty thousand opera devotees in Tokyo alone. So far they have seen little besides the conventional productions of such operas as *Boris Godunov* or *Così Fan Tutte,* but lately, original Japanese works have appeared. Ikuma Dan's *Twilight Crane* is the operatic version of Junji Kinoshita's hit play based on the folk tale of a crane whose life is saved by a farmer; she turns into a woman and out of gratitude becomes his bride. The love story of Townsend Harris, America's first consul in Japan, and the geisha O-Kichi is the theme of Kosaku Yamada's *The Black Ships*. Osamu Shimizu has adapted to the opera form a Kabuki play about a maker of masks, called *Tale of Shuzen Temple*. And Yamada is in the process of completing yet another Japanese opera to be called *Princess Fragrance*.

In contrast to this tendency, the number of vocal and instrumental recitals has sharply dropped. As a result of visits by such artists as Traubel, Huesch, Cortot, Gieseking, Heifetz, and Backhaus, listeners have, for the time being, lost interest in recitals of Western music by Japanese artists. Tickets for the concerts of the famous foreigners sell for a minimum of 500 yen and a maximum of 3,000—far too much for an average Japanese, who earns about 20,000 yen (roughly $55) a month. Yet students, often the most ardent followers of Western music, will carefully save up money in order to attend performances of these visiting artists, and such expressions as "my Cortot savings," or "my Heifetz savings," are often heard.

Traditional Japanese music, which has a history that goes back hundreds of years, and still retains, in the Imperial Court, such magnificent survivals as Gagaku, orchestral music dating from the eighth and ninth centuries and originally imported from the mainland of Asia, is a more or less private art. Apart from the great music that accompanies the puppet plays and Kabuki, there are few public performances of music alone. Geisha songs are of course accompanied on the samisen [a three-stringed banjolike instrument], and in upper class houses, the koto (an instrument that resembles the zither) is studied by the daughters as part of their education and refinement. It is believed that to learn the koto and flower arrangement before marriage gives depth to a girl's sentiments. However, the most famous koto players have been men, and one of the very few Japanese artists who can command a large audience for native music is Michio Miyagi, the greatest koto player and composer of new pieces on old themes and in old styles.

Among workers of the lower classes, Naniwabushi, a musical storytelling which is a survival of an ancient form, is the most popular musical expression. These are usually sung in a strained and hoarse voice and tell of the heroic and desperate actions of warriors and their followers. The general effect of Naniwabushi is that of an American Western sung as a ballad. Several times a year, some ten famous singers of this type give a huge performance in Tokyo; the majority of their spellbound audience consists of older people.

The most rapidly growing and the most hectic of the recent additions to Japan's popular entertainment is American and South American jazz. It is sweeping the country and finding its chief devotees among the young people between seventeen and twenty-five years of age. In special jazz cafés they whistle, stomp, and become intoxicated by the intense rhythms. The older people tend to frown on this new jazz craze, and wonder what has become of the old Japanese songs. But the jazz mania shows no sign of being halted, and may in the future acquire as great a hold on the Japanese as it now appears to have on Westerners.

Unlike the films, where native style is gaining ground, the predominant influence of the West on Japanese music seems likely to continue.

NIPPON WITH A NEW FACE [6]

The bespectacled diplomat in the hotel-room chair seemed amused at my question: Why, in a country noted for government by assassination, had there been no serious attempt in ten years to kill a Japanese or United States official? "Lack of enthusiasm," he said in precise English. "Young people feel social changes can be achieved without resorting to this primitive and ineffective method, while the general public, it would seem, has greatly lost interest in politics."

He glanced down to where his empty right trouser leg was tucked into his belt. The leg had been blown off by a Korean assassin's bomb in 1932.

This was Japanese Foreign Minister Mamoru Shigemitsu, sixty-eight, who served in two wartime cabinets, signed the surrender aboard the battleship Missouri, spent five years in prison for helping wage offensive war. . . . Shigemitsu is a remarkably durable barometer of his country's world standing: he and Japan alike have come through ten years of ruin, retribution and recovery.

Today the once-sprawling empire of Japan is reduced to four main islands. . . . It is engaged in a frantic, endless race to balance its exports against imports of food and raw materials. . . .

Yet for all that, this vulnerable, picture-post-card country, little more than a decade after its crushing defeat in war, again boasts the biggest industry in the Far East and with it holds the balance of power in Asia. A Japan harnessed to Russia and Red China could lure what is left of independent Asia into the Red camp and tip the scales fatally against the West. A prosperous Japan on the side of the free world remains a valuable ally.

[6] From "Japan," article by Peter Kalischer, author and CBS correspondent in Japan. *Collier's*. 137:58-67. March 2, 1956. Reprinted by permission.

Seizing or subverting Japan is therefore the Communists' jack pot in East Asia; keeping Japan our ally is America's first concern there; and getting the most for the best—from both sides if possible—is Japan's.

For seven occupation years the Japanese had no choice of sides. We ran the country and fed them slabs of democracy sandwiched between $2.5 million worth of relief and rehabilitation. Japan enjoyed our help and even digested a good deal of the democracy. But when the occupation lid came off in 1952 it revealed a country weary of being told what to do, curious to taste the forbidden fruit beyond the bamboo curtain, and relishing its authority over the foreigners who had been giving it orders for so long.

The new Japan is fermenting a mash of new ideas and old customs. It is mixing political democracy with feudal loyalties, free enterprise with giant monopolies, and several shades of Marxism with a hankering for the good old days. The nation that once meekly did what a handful of leaders told it to is now outspokenly divided on every major issue — American troops and bases, rearmament, relations with Red countries, neutrality, foreign trade.

Japan is on her feet—but headed where?

Postwar Changes

In searching for the answer I took a long, fresh look at the country I first saw as a GI more than ten years ago and have worked in most of the time since. Once-devastated cities—Tokyo, Yokohama, Nagoya, Osaka, Hiroshima—show hardly a scar. Phalanxes of new office buildings, new apartment houses and plaster-front shops cover ground only recently bare of everything but fire-proof safes and brick chimneys. From the southern tip of Kyushu to the fishing villages of northern Hokkaido farmers have harvested a record rice crop. Handkerchief-size plots are still cultivated like truck gardens, but the machine age is creeping in; a few farmers' wives now own washing machines — something newsworthy enough to get their pictures in the paper.

The Dai-Ichi Building in Tokyo, General MacArthur's famed command post, has reverted to the insurance company which owns it. Crowds bunch around store-window TV screens instead of queuing up for rations. Gay print dresses and Italian hairdos are the vogue among girls whose elder sisters wore baggy wartime slacks. And the girls are walking *"avec"*—that is, with their escorts, arm in arm, instead of behind them. (They borrowed the word from the French but the habit from the GI's.)

Millions of Japanese spend more money in pinball parlors than the government does on national defense. For businessmen, the golf course vies with the geisha house as the place to seal a deal. In any city you can take your pick of Japanese, American, French or British movies. The All Girl Revue is at the Tokyo Takarazuka Theatre, formerly the Ernie Pyle, formerly the Takarazuka. The burlesques feature battalions of classic stripteasers and one new variety—a young lady shedding a kimono.

Fewer than one hundred rickshas are left on Tokyo's streets, which now are choked with 8 million people, 25,000 private cars, 12,000 taxis, enormous diesel buses, motorcycle-powered three-wheelers, and bike-riding delivery boys balancing anything from eight tiers of noodle soup to a plate-glass window. There is a major traffic accident every thirty minutes.

The *Asahi,* Japan's largest newspaper (circulation 5 million), now runs news bulletins in English, along with Japanese, on its moving electric signboard, New York *Times* style. Throughout the country English is the second language, American products the technological yardstick, Marxism the religion of the intellectuals, mambo the latest dance craze and baseball, introduced seventy-two years ago, still the most popular sport. One hundred thousand Tokyoites turned out in the rain last fall to greet the New York Yankees—and the young man who carried a Yankee Go Home placard on May Day was more than likely among them.

The Emperor

Probably the most extraordinary sight in postwar Japan is Emperor Hirohito—for the very reason that he can now be seen. Up to a decade ago the Japanese people bowed low and averted their eyes even when the Imperial Presence passed in a speeding train or car. They would not have dared look at the awesome descendant of the world's oldest unbroken imperial dynasty. When they raised their heads after the war and looked straight at him, the Japanese saw an unassuming little man with a toothbrush mustache, thick glasses, a shy smile and a hesitant walk. Japanese eyes are still a little blurred by the image of the prewar emperor, but they genuinely love the one they see now. Not even the Communists dare suggest openly, as they did right after the war, that he be abolished.

Nowadays nobody apologizes to the emperor by kneeling in the Imperial Palace Plaza, or, as happened on the day of surrender, by committing group hara-kiri. But sixteen persons were crushed to death on the double span bridge leading into the palace grounds when a crowd of 380,000 came to pay their New Year's respects in 1954; and thousands of countrywomen still troop into Tokyo to sweep the palace grounds in a labor of love.

The man who inspires this devotion is a curious mixture of ancient tradition and modern tastes. Hirohito wears only Western clothes, prefers European cooking, and sleeps on a bed instead of a Japanese-style straw mat or tatami. He makes regular public appearances, and has informal pictures taken by the court photographer. He has fought a slow battle against the imperial household's 930 retainers, headed by a grand chamberlain, who have controlled his life since babyhood. . . .

Still, there is strong conservative sentiment to enshrine Hirohito again—and he might be unable to resist it.

American Influence

America, more than any other nation, has had a hand in shaping modern Japan. History brought Commodore Matthew Perry into Tokyo Bay a century ago and General Douglas MacArthur there ninety-two years later to fulfill a prophecy by Perry that ranks as one of the shrewdest pieces of long-range forecasting ever made.

To me [Perry wrote] it seems that the people of America will extend their dominion and power until they shall have brought within their mighty embrace multitudes of the islands of the great Pacific, and placed the Saxon race upon the eastern shores of Asia. And I think, too, that eastward and southward will her great rival in future aggrandizement (Russia) stretch forth her power to the coasts of China and Siam; and thus the Saxon and the Cossack will meet once more, in strife or in friendship, on another field. Will it be friendship? I fear not!

Almost from the beginning, MacArthur's occupation wrestled with this problem in a modern context: disarming and reforming an aggressor Japan and at the same time building up a solvent ally which could resist the growing Communist menace next door.

Under a broad State-War-Navy Department memorandum dated August 29, 1945, General MacArthur attempted more social changes in two and a half years than Japan had seen in the previous fifty. He disarmed the Japanese down to the last KP, arrested high-ranking military and civilian jingoists, encouraged labor to organize, purged 200,000 persons (including Japan's . . . premier, Ichiro Hatoyama, and twelve of his sixteen-man cabinet), abolished Shinto as the state religion, dissolved the zaibatsu—the family cartels—, revamped the education system, remodeled the judiciary, decentralized the police force, gave women equal civil rights, and carried out a land-reform program so successful the Communists tried to claim the credit. The Japanese also were induced to adopt a new American-model constitution which renounced war and declared that "land, sea and air forces, as well as other war potential, will never be maintained."

As the cold war grew hotter, reconstruction took precedence over reform. By mid-1948, MacArthur was banning large-scale political strikes that were wrecking recovery.

The following year trust-busting ended, and the big zaibatsu firms he split began rolling back into one like balls of quicksilver. Inflation was halted by rigorous austerity and mass government firings.

When left-wing labor indulged in sporadic sabotage and violence, MacArthur purged from unions and then from public life Communist leaders whom he had liberated as political prisoners in 1945. With the Korean war, Communist publications were suppressed and key industries told to fire known Communist employees. The same year the first of the early purgees were depurged. Then, with all his occupation forces ticketed for Korea, MacArthur set Japan on the road to rearmament by ordering the government to form a 75,000-man National Police Reserve. Every nation, he declared, has the inherent right of self-defense.

By the time the occupation ended in April 1952, nearly every stratum of Japanese society had got a pat and a kick. Now, four years later, many are outspoken about its policies and their effects.

"I had to report to the police once a month for a year because I didn't surrender my family's samurai sword," said Tetsu Nakamura, of Kyoto. "Now you want us to build jet fighters."

Labor unions organized under the occupation accuse us of having revived the military and siding with the old order. Businessmen criticize early trust-busting and labor reforms that raised the price of Japanese products on the world market. Conservatives chide us for initially "encouraging" Communism. "The Communists you let out of jail were *not* political prisoners," Foreign Minister Shigemitsu told me. "They were common criminals in prison for breaking laws."

The average Japanese—if there is one—will admit we behaved far better than the Russians would have, or (some say frankly) than the Japanese under similar circumstances. But we, not the Russians, are in Japan today—135,000 United States servicemen in 600 installations—and the Japanese have a haunting sensation that the occupation never ended. They called the old occupation troops *Shin-chu-gun* — advance army; they call our present security forces *Chu-ryu-gun*—the army that stays. . . .

Current Japanese Attitudes

Defeat in war and the physical and psychological destruction of the military caste have helped turn most Japanese into pacifists. The country's two big postwar best sellers are violently antimilitary. One called *Long the Imperial Way* relates the brutalized life of the Japanese enlisted man in China. The hero of the other, *Homecoming,* is a cashiered navy officer who copes with his problems better than his conventional fellow officers.

But the main reason most Japanese want no part of war is the obvious one—they were atom-bombed twice. In 1946, I called on a top Japanese nuclear scientist, Professor R. Sagane of Tokyo Imperial University, now dead, and asked what he thought about Japan rearming in the future. "Useless," he told me. "Today there is no such thing as a good second- or third-class military force. Without atomic weapons a nation might as well not have any."

That argument has gained ground since two former enemies are now armed with the H-bomb. The Japanese are understandably touchy on the subject—106,000 of them died in just two old-fashioned nuclear explosions. Fate also chose twenty-three Japanese fishermen to be the first victims of an H-bomb fall-out near Bikini in March 1954. The "ashes of death" incident, for which we paid $2 million compensation, brought Japanese-American relations to a postwar low. . . . [See "Japan and the H-Bomb," in Section IV, below.—Eds.]

If there is one personal history that shows the new face of Japan it is that of thirty-year-old Tadashi Itagaki. Itagaki graduated from the Japanese Air Force Academy in March 1945, was sent to Korea as a second lieutenant pilot in June and was taken prisoner by the

Russians in August. In July 1948, he was moved to a camp in Khabarovsk, Siberia, which held four hundred Japanese enlisted men and three hundred low-ranking officers. By the time Itagaki got there a social revolution had taken place. A small group, supplied with books, pamphlets and a Japanese-language newspaper which gave the news according to Moscow, had converted most of the men to communism. Enlisted men would surround an officer and badger him until he tore off his insignia. "After three years, do you still want to fight wars?" they would jeer. "Japan doesn't even have an army." Itagaki held out for six months. He was a fervent believer in the emperor system, and he had another special reason: his father was Lieutenant General Seishiro Itagaki, one of Japan's most aggressive militarists.

One day a fellow prisoner came up to him waving a copy of the Japanese newspaper.

"Great news today," he said. "Tojo and your **father** and five other war criminals were executed in Tokyo."

"To me," Itagaki recently explained, "my father was almost synonymous with the emperor. When I heard the news my world collapsed. I thought if this could happen, then Japan was really turning inside out, as the Communists among us said."

The next day Itagaki joined the Communists.

In 1950 he was repatriated. The Communists lionized him; they tried to use him as a speaker in an election campaign.

But something was wrong. The picture of Japan that Itagaki had inside his head did not jibe with the Japan he had come back to.

"I talked with my mother and my friends," Itagaki said, "and I read the new constitution. Then I made up my mind."

Six months after his return he quit the party. Today he is a very ordinary young man with a very ordinary job he wants to keep. He is not much interested in politics, but he votes Right Socialist.

"I think Japan should be friends with everybody," he said. "I don't want any more war."

II. GOVERNMENT AND POLITICS

The foundations of the present parliamentary system of government in Japan were laid by the 1947 constitution. Largely written by General MacArthur's staff advisers, the constitution was designed to erase old political forms in Japan, notably the institution of the emperor, and to replace them by a government based on popular representation. Thus, it provides for the separation of powers (executive, legislative, and judicial) as in the American system, with real power resting in the Diet as the legislative arm of government.

In studying postwar Japanese political development it is important to keep in mind the fact that the constitution inaugurated a form of government basically dissimilar to that of prewar Japan—which was in effect ruled by an oligarchy of powerful groups among the aristocracy and the army. While democracy and the party system appear to be functioning well in Japan, dissatisfaction is shown by a move to revise the constitution. And there are forces at work that would undermine it entirely.

This section opens with a discussion by Hugh Borton of the nature of democracy in modern Japan and the chances for its future. A short article outlines the structure of the present government. A list of the postwar prime ministers with their terms of office is given to orient the reader. An article taken from an introduction to Japan sketches the history and character of the major political parties. The origins and nature of the extreme right in Japan are taken up in an article on ultranationalist groups. The composition and character of the Japanese Communist party are discussed in an article by Rodger Swearingen. This is followed by biographical sketches of the two most prominent postwar prime ministers, Yoshida and Hatoyama.

DEMOCRACY IN JAPAN [1]

In any analysis of the growth of democracy in modern times in Japan, it is important to remember that in the years immediately following the restoration of power to the Emperor Meiji in January 1868 the new leaders devoted their main strength and effort to the solution of their country's economic dilemma. The problems which absorbed their time and energy were practical ones; political problems began to demand their dominant attention only after many of the basic economic issues had been settled. The new imperial government had been established in 1868 by some of the most powerful feudal barons and their warrior-advisers, who had rallied around the youthful emperor.

These men formed a small group of oligarchs who were the *de facto* rulers as councillors and state ministers. They improvised a national governmental structure and operated within a framework of broad policies proclaimed by the emperor. They promised to establish a public assembly and to lay great stress on public discussion. In reality, however, these oligarchs were more interested in stifling public discussion than in encouraging it. By 1881, they laid down the broad principles for the constitution which were incorporated in that document.

The constitution, which had been drafted in secret by the oligarchs, was promulgated on February 11, 1889,

[1] From "Past Limitations and the Future of Democracy in Japan," article by Hugh Borton, president of Haverford College. *Political Science Quarterly*. 70:410-20. September 1955. Reprinted by permission.

by Emperor Meiji who proclaimed it as the immutable, fundamental law for his subjects and their descendants. For fifty-eight years, from that day until May 3, 1947, when the post-World War II constitution went into force, not a single change was made in the document or in the central concept that the emperor be the center, the axis, of constitutional monarchy. It established the emperor as sacred and inviolable. It gave legal sanction to the wide powers previously exercised for him by his ministers. It granted extensive authority to the executive branch of the government and limited the legislative and judicial branches. The extra-legal institutions such as the Elder Statesmen (Genrō) who acted as imperial advisers only increased the powers of the emperor as the chief executive. . . . The concept of the state as an overriding entity prevailed. The government rested on the suzerainty of the crown, not on the discretion of a parliamentary body. . . .

Thus, from the restoration to power of Emperor Meiji in 1868 to the surrender by the representatives of his grandson to General MacArthur on September 2, 1945, conservatism, absolutism and a strong, centralized autocracy were the guiding political principles of Japan. The Potsdam Declaration of July 26, 1945, on which the surrender was based, had stated that the occupation of Japan would continue until "there has been established, in accordance with the freely expressed will of the Japanese people, a peacefully inclined and responsible government." In other words, two of the basic objectives of the United States and its allies for postwar Japan were the creation of conditions which would prevent Japan from becoming a military menace and which would assure, to the extent that it was possible to do so, the creation of democratic institutions in Japan.

Reforms During the Occupation

Many of the directives issued by the Supreme Commander for the Allied Powers (SCAP), especially those during the first two years of the occupation, were directed at achieving this democratization. In other words, certain essential reforms were undertaken to create an atmosphere in which democracy would prosper. While demobilization of the Japanese Army and Navy was being effected, human rights were protected by order of the supreme commander. Restrictions on freedom of the press and radio, except on material critical of the occupation, were removed. Bans were lifted on political, civil and religious liberties. Discrimination was forbidden on grounds of race, nationality, creed or political opinion. Political prisoners were released and the national police were stripped of their authoritarian powers.

But if democracy was to have a chance for permanent survival, it was necessary for Japan to have a new constitution based on democratic principles. For the first five months of the occupation, desultory attempts at constitutional revision were undertaken by the conservative political leaders. Early in February 1946, however, officials of General MacArthur's headquarters prepared a draft for a new constitution which stripped the emperor of governmental powers and strengthened the legislative and judicial branches of the government. Civil rights were guaranteed; the cabinet was made collectively responsible to the Diet. The latter was made the sole lawmaking body and had complete control over the budget. On the insistence of General MacArthur, the document also contained a provision which abolished war as a sovereign right of the nation. The final draft for the new constitution, which contained all of these provisions of the MacArthur draft, was accepted by the Japanese cabinet in March 1946. After the addition of a few changes which strengthened the democratic aspects of the document, it was approved by the Diet on November 3, 1946. When it was implemented by new legislation strengthening the new freedom and liberty of the Japanese people, the formal framework, at least, was at hand for Japan's democratization.

Other reforms encouraged or initiated by the occupation also contributed toward the possibility that Japan would not revert to its old conservative autocratic ways. For example, encouragement was given to the rise of a strong labor movement. After the passage of legislation which legalized collective bargaining and trade unions, union membership jumped in twelve months from about 125,000 to 4.5 million. . . .

Many other occupation-inspired reforms, such as the abolition of absentee landownership, the purge of ultra-nationalist leaders in the political and economic field, and the deconcentration of economic and financial power, were directed against past autocratic practices. Two changes, of special significance, occurred in the police system and in national education. Since the Japanese police, who had been controlled by the home minister and had wide powers, had been one of the important elements in forming a pre-surrender dictatorial government, their overhaul was imperative. After temporary objections by the Japanese cabinet to a proposal from General MacArthur's headquarters for complete decentralization of police powers, a new police law was finally enacted on December 17, 1947. This law adopted the principle of decentralization by dividing the police into local municipal police and national rural police. The former were to be controlled by local police boards, the latter by a National Public Safety Commission. Other functions formerly exercised by the police were transferred to either the local or national governments. Police, customs and patrol duties in Japanese territorial waters were assumed by a Maritime Safety Authority. Thus, one of the strongest agencies of Japanese totalitarianism was transformed to make it as difficult as possible to use it for the establishment of a police state.

As for educational reform, in prewar days, the Ministry of Education in Tokyo exercised autocratic control over the entire educational system, from primary school to university, and the schools became important outlets for the transmission of nationalist dogma and militarism. The whole system was designed to discourage individual initiative and independent thinking and to foster conformity and absolute obedience. If the obstacles to the revival and strengthening of democratic tendencies among the Japanese were to be removed, as provided in the Potsdam Declaration of 1945, an educational system and philosophy diametrically opposed to that which existed before surrender would have to be evolved.

The first important step in educational reforms came in October 1945 when the schools were opened, but militaristic and nationalistic subjects were not permitted to be taught and a program of screening teachers and revising the textbooks was undertaken. The 1946 New Year's Day statement of the emperor was another important event in educational reform. It denied his divinity and the superiority of the Japanese over other people and urged that wisdom and knowledge be sought abroad. By the time the new constitution went into effect in May 1947, the entire educational system had been completely reformed to the extent that this could be achieved by legislation. New laws stressed the importance of individual initiative and inquiry and guaranteed academic freedom. Education was made compulsory for nine years. The most significant administrative change was in the decentralization of control through the formation of local, elective school boards responsible to the local community. Theoretically, at least, the minister of education in Tokyo could no longer act as a dictator over the whole system or be subject to the dictates of the party or group in power.

Weaknesses of Occupation Reforms

But helpful as these and many other reforms might be to facilitate Japan's democratization, they had two basic weaknesses. In the first place, the innovations were carried out during a military occupation. Though they were formally implemented by the Japanese Diet and cabinet, the initiative had come from the various staff officers of General MacArthur's headquarters. Though many leading Japanese had been consulted in formulating these new policies, General MacArthur as the supreme commander could always exercise a direct or indirect veto on actions which he did not approve, or order the Japanese government to carry out policies which he considered urgent. In other words, even though the reforms were accepted formally, there was no assurance that they had been wholeheartedly accepted by the Japanese people. The test would come only after the occupation ceased.

The second weakness of these reforms was the fact that in Japanese history the men who control the government and their ideas have been far more important than the formal structure through which they operated. The Meiji Constitution of 1889 was made to fit the beliefs, ambitions and desires of the Meiji leaders. They made the various government officers work for them; they were in no sense bound by "the will of the people." Consequently, if we are to evaluate correctly the future possibilities of the democratization of Japan, we must conclude our analysis with a brief account of the governments which operated in postwar Japan and of the trend which has developed particularly after April 28, 1952, when the peace treaty came into effect.

As for Japan's postwar political development, while there have been various changes in party names and in political alignments, there are three general groups. On the right are the two largest parties, the Liberal and Democratic parties, which, despite their official names, are basically conservative. In the center and left of center is the Socialist party or Social Democrats who have split into a right and left wing. On the left are the Communists, theoretical Marxists and fellow travelers.

From the surrender of Japan on September 2, 1945 to the elections of February 1955, there have been ten cabinets and five general elections for the House of Representatives. Five of these cabinets have been headed by Shigeru Yoshida for a total of seven out of ten years. For about half of the time that he was premier, his Liberal party had an absolute majority in the House of Representatives. After the elections in April 1953, he retained control of the government through a shaky coalition but was finally forced to resign in December 1954. He was succeeded by Ichiro Hatoyama, president of the Democratic party. In the elections in February 1955, the Democrats won the largest number of seats in the House of Representatives and Hatoyama was subsequently confirmed as prime minister.

A significant aspect of Japan's modern political trend is the fact that the electorate has always preferred conservative candidates. Although the Liberal and Progressive parties may not have agreed on the question of who should control the parties, they are both conservative and together have possessed more than half of the votes in the House of Representatives. Even in the election of April 1947, after which Tetsu Katayama, a Social Democrat, formed a cabinet, the Socialists controlled less than one third of the seats. Furthermore, after the unexpectedly heavy Communist vote in the elections in January 1949, when they polled nearly 10 per cent of the total and returned thirty-five members to Parliament, their support has rapidly declined. For example, in February 1955, the Communists elected only two representatives to Parliament. Apparently many former supporters of the Communists shifted to the Left-wing Socialists who increased their strength by one fifth. Together with the Right-wing Socialists they control one third of the seats in the House of Representatives. But the combined seats of the two conservative parties equal nearly two thirds of the total.

Postwar Reaction

In view of this basic conservative political atmosphere in postwar Japan, therefore, it is not surprising to find signs of a shift in the direction the nation is headed. In fact, there is general support, stimulated by a new nationalism which has arisen since the peace treaty went into effect in April 1952, for shelving many of the reforms established under the occupation. To verify this generalization, we need only glance at what has been happening to the reforms mentioned above. In the first place, the basic civil rights inaugurated by General MacArthur and guaranteed by the constitution have been severely threatened by two parallel developments, namely, the passage of an anti-subversive activity law and the return to centralized police control. As for the former, Premier Yoshida pressed for the passage of a law which would control the terroristic activities of extremists, especially the Communists and Communist-inspired organizations. The proposed law was so worded, however, as to be applicable to labor unions and political parties which "incited or agitated" political action. Consequently, it was strenuously opposed by organized labor and by many of Yoshida's political opponents who feared that a rigid enforcement of the law would threaten individual freedoms. On the basis of a new fear of communism aroused by the May Day riots in 1952 and a promise from the attorney general that care would be taken in applying the law, however, Yoshida obtained approval of the law in July 1952.

An even greater threat to Japan's democratization has been the basic alteration in the reforms of the police system. The chief purpose of the SCAP-inspired reforms was to prevent the police from continuing to be an enforcement agency directly under the cabinet which could use them for its own ends. Prime Minister Yoshida, in the face of Communist disturbances and protracted strikes, maintained that the dual system of municipal and national rural police was inefficient and incapable of dealing with internal peace and security. He proposed, therefore, that many of the changes inaugurated during the occupation be abandoned and that a national police system under the supervision of a Central Police Board responsible directly to the Prime Minister be established. He also recommended that police chiefs in the various prefectures be named by the Chairman of the Police Board and that they be national government employees. In February 1953, Parliament refused to consider the national budget unless Yoshida withdrew his proposal. Finally, in June 1954, after the Socialists had boycotted the Lower House, the conservative majority approved the new bill. Consequently, the police in small communities and the five largest cities in the country lost their autonomy and were again placed in a position to enforce the will of the government and to threaten democratization.

The movement to revise or reconsider the constitution, which has notably gained momentum . . . is more complicated than the other issues which are demanding current reconsideration. The main question of revision centers on the question of rearmament and is complicated by the reversal of the American position on that issue. Most Japanese realize that it was General MacArthur who insisted in February 1946 that the constitution contain a provision (Article IX) prohibiting Japan from maintaining armed forces. They also know that there has been an increased tendency on the part of American officials to emphasize the role Japan could play in the defense against communism. For example, Vice President Nixon stated in December 1953 that the United States was mistaken in its earlier policy and that the Japanese National Safety forces, which were planned at over 110,000 men, were not enough.

In the meantime, the question whether the constitution should be amended has been made a political issue. The Progressives, and their successors, the Democrats, urged such action and the formation of regular armed forces. Premier Yoshida argued that since the proposed forces were to be defensive they were not unconstitutional. Another aspect of revision of the constitution is the position taken by some of the old nationalists who

were influential members of the Manchuria clique. . . .
[Nobusuke] Kishi [the present premier], one of the
former directors of the General Affairs Bureau of Man-
chukuo, recently declared that "the time is here for a
wholesale scrutiny of the constitution." His remarks
become even more ominous for the future of democracy
in Japan when it is realized that he served as minister of
commerce and industry under Tojo's cabinet . . . and
that in November 1954 he acted as chief mediator between the dissident Yoshida followers and the organizers
of the new conservative Democratic party.

Finally, a reversion to prewar educational policies is
a further indication of the present trend away from democratization in Japan. While Prime Minister, Yoshida
sponsored this reversal of Allied policy and a shift
toward centralization for financial and political reasons.
The war damage repairs and replacement of school
buildings were too great a burden for local communities
to bear. At the same time, the central government
sought ways to control the Left-wing-dominated Teachers Union. Previous efforts to restrict the political activity of this important union had failed, so a bill was
proposed to place teachers on the payroll of the national
government. As government employees, they would be
prohibited from political activity and the Teachers Union
could be controlled. Moreover, the law provided that the
power of appointment of teachers should revert to the
Ministry of Education. The Yoshida government was
severely attacked by the teachers and the press for con-
sciously attempting to destroy the liberalizing effect of
the occupational policies. As the *Asahi*, one of Tokyo's
leading papers, editorialized, "Passage of these laws will
have a more far-reaching effect on the freedom of education and perhaps on other freedoms now enjoyed by

the people than any other legislation since the war." Consequently, when these new laws were approved early in 1954, centralized control of the entire educational system was possible.

Under the premiership of Hatoyama, the trend away from the Allied policies which aimed at assisting the process of democratization and toward authoritarian control is likely to continue. The by-products of this trend also cannot be overlooked. A rearmament movement and the revitalization of the armed forces give ample opportunity for the old militarists or their protégés to reassert themselves as a significant nationalist influence. The reemergence of the large financial combines (the Zaibatsu) and the rationalization of industry [organization on an orderly and economic basis] facilitate a close alliance between the government and the leading financiers. The concentration of police power and educational policies within the cabinet make regimentation possible if not probable.

Balance of Forces

But over against this discouraging prognosis are arrayed new forces which will retard the trend toward totalitarian control and may even reverse it. First, the labor movement has come of age and the unions have tasted the giddying effect of political power. They and their members will not easily give up their freedom of action. Secondly, the agrarian reforms, which affected a large portion of the population, have lifted a heavy debt burden from many farm families. As a result, they are reluctant to see a return to prewar conditions for fear that they may lose what they have already gained. In the third place, the equality of the sexes, guaranteed by the constitution, has released an entirely new force. Women are coming into their own. They are equal before the law, vote, work, and have greater educational opportunities than ever before. No politician will dare to deprive them of their rights. Finally, the bitter pill of defeat confronted many Japanese, particularly the youth, with a new political philosophy to guide them; those who have found it in democracy do not intend to give it up.

On balance, therefore, prospects for democratization are not as bright as they appeared to be before the Treaty of Peace was signed, but it is unlikely that authoritarianism will be able to negate the advances already made. The reactions against the occupation-inspired reforms are natural ones and in the end Japan may settle down to a moderate form of democracy well to the right of center.

STRUCTURE OF GOVERNMENT [2]

The main characteristics of the new constitution, particularly in contrast with the old one, are as follows: (1) the symbolization of the state by the emperor and recognition of popular sovereignty, (2) renunciation of war, (3) superiority of the House of Representatives over the House of Councillors and (4) the assumption by the cabinet of responsibility to the Diet. . . .

Executive

Japan has adopted the parliamentary system of government, under which the executive and the legislature are not as independent of each other as under the United States governmental system. The prime minister

[2] From "Japan as It Is Today," pamphlet published by Public Information and Cultural Affairs Bureau, Japanese Ministry of Foreign Affairs. Tokyo. 1956. p21-3. Reprinted by permission.

in Japan is designated from among the members of the Diet by the action of that body. All cabinet members must be civilians, and at least half of them must be selected from the Diet, to which they are collectively answerable. If the House of Representatives passes a non-confidence resolution, or rejects a confidence resolution, the cabinet must either resign en masse or dissolve the House within ten days. . . .

For the purpose of local administration, Japan is divided into forty-six districts. Under these regional governmental organizations are the city, town and village units. Local government personnel totaled 1,391,368 in April 1956.

Diet

The Diet is the highest organ of state power and the only lawmaking body. It consists of two Houses, the House of Representatives (467 seats) and the House of Councillors (250 seats). . . .

The members in the House of Representatives are elected for a four-year term. But their term of office can be terminated whenever the House is dissolved. The electorate system for the House of Representatives is based on the medium constituency. The members in the House of Councillors are elected for a six-year term. One half of the total membership of the House of Councillors are elected every three years. One hundred out of the 250-member House of Councillors stand election on the national constituency while the rest are elected from the local constituencies.

Voters in all elections must be Japanese nationals, both men and women, who are twenty years of age or over. . . .

Judiciary

Judicial power is vested in a supreme court and in lower courts. All judges are permitted full independence in the exercise of their conscience and they are bound only by the constitution and the laws.

The supreme court is composed of a chief justice and fourteen judges. The chief justice is appointed by the emperor as designated by the cabinet and all other judges are appointed by the cabinet, but reviewed by the people.

PRIME MINISTERS OF JAPAN
SINCE THE PROMULGATION OF THE
1947 CONSTITUTION [3]

Tetsu Katayama, Socialist
  May 1947-March 1948

Hitoshi Ashida, Democrat
  March 1948-October 1948

Shigeru Yoshida, Liberal, second term
  October-December 1948
  (First term: May 1946-May 1947)

Shigeru Yoshida, third term
  January 1949-August 1952

Shigeru Yoshida, fourth term
  August 1952-April 1953

Shigeru Yoshida, fifth term
  May 1953-November 1954

Ichiro Hatoyama, Japan Democrat
  December 1954-March 1955

Ichiro Hatoyama, second term
  March 1955-October 1955

[3] Compiled by the Information Office, Consulate General of Japan, New York. October 1957.

Ichiro Hatoyama, third term
    November 1955-November 1956
Tanzan Ishibashi, Liberal-Democrat
    December 1956-February 1957
Nobusuke Kishi, Liberal Democrat
    February 1957-

THE JAPANESE POLITICAL PARTIES [4]

Before the war Japan's two leading political parties
were the Seiyûkai and Minsei-tô. With the revival of
party government in the autumn of 1945, both reappeared to become the leading conservative parties, the
former as the Liberal party and the latter as the Progressive party. Meanwhile, members of former proletarian parties organized the Japan Social Democratic
party, and the Communist party came out of hiding
with the return from exile or release from prison of its
former leaders. A profusion of minor parties ranged
from right to left behind candidates of widely varying
backgrounds and degrees of political experience. In the
1946 general elections, 267 parties entered candidates.
An inevitable weeding out of most of the minor parties
and splits or consolidations of the more vigorous of them
have made for a gradual simplification of the party
scene. Since late in 1955 there have been two main
parties, which between them have filled all but a handful
of seats in the lower house and three quarters of those
in the upper house. Backgrounds, policies, and personalities of the major parties are as follows.

A. The Japan Socialist party (Nihon Shakai-tô).
Pre-occupation suppression of the socialist movement

[4] From *An Introduction to Japan*, by Herschel Webb, instructor in Chinese
and Japanese at Columbia University. Columbia University Press. New York.
1957. p54-8. Reprinted by permission.

gave the Japanese left wing a cohesiveness under stress that it was not long to maintain after it was freed for political activity. Early solidarity of the Social Democratic party (Shakai Minshu-tô) led to unexpected strength at the polls in April 1947, followed by strong positions for the party in the two succeeding coalition cabinets under their own leader Tetsu Katayama, from May 1947, until March 1948, and under Prime Minister Ashida, a Progressive, until October 1948. Yet there came to be fundamental differences between extremists and moderates within the party. In October 1951, the two wings split. The immediate issue was Japanese ratification of a peace treaty in the drafting of which neither the Soviet Union nor China had participated. Right Wingers, though they opposed the United States-Japanese defense pact that accompanied the treaty, supported the treaty itself. This the Left Wing refused to do. The Right Wing took a firm stand against rearmament, but avoided commitment to outright anti-Americanism.

Meanwhile, Left-Wing Socialists maintained strict opposition to cooperation with the West in all phases of its struggle with world communism. It opposed active and passive aid to the South Korean cause during the Korean War and after the war favored complete withdrawal of foreign defense troops from Japanese soil. At the same time it staunchly resisted rearmament for Japan either with or without amendment of the constitution. Such a program attracted some of Japan's neutralists, to whom commitment on either side of the cold war seemed ill-advised, but it also appealed to those committed on the side of communism who were not actually Communist party members.

Relaxation of American-Soviet tension in 1955 had the effect of diminishing some of the issues between the two wings, and in October 1955 they merged to form the Japan Socialist party. Mosaburo Suzuki, leader of the Left Wing, became party chairman, while Right-Wing leader Inejiro Asanuma became chief secretary. Some disagreements still remain among factions of the party, though all of them agree on an anti-capitalistic program of domestic economy and a greater or lesser degree of opposition to the pro-American foreign program of the majority party. Socialists hold less than a third of the seats in the House of Representatives, but their program has powerful support among labor unions and in intellectual circles.

B. The Liberal-Democratic party (Jiyû-Minshu-tô). Japan's present majority party is basically conservative and favors alliance with the West. It came into being in November 1955, with the union of the Liberal and Democratic parties. The latter had consisted of the members of the old Progressive party plus dissidents from the Liberals. Postwar conservative factions exhibit at least one of the striking characteristics of their prewar counterparts: they unify not so much around articulated programs or policies as behind dominating politicians. Personality clashes among conservative leaders delayed formation of a united party until after reconciliation of the Left- and Right-Wing Socialists had made it a political necessity. These clashes have continued to plague the new party since its establishment. It remains to be seen whether the union will be stable.

In March 1957, Nobusuke Kishi, who became prime minister on February 25, was made head of the party.

C. The Ryokufû-kai. In 1947 a group of House of Councillors members of generally conservative political philosophy formed a separate party known as the Ryokufû-kai, or "Green Breeze Society." Its importance to

Japanese political life lies in the fact that its upper-house membership of thirty-one seats prevents either of the major parties from obtaining majority control in the House of Councillors. The Ryokufû-kai fared badly in the elections of July 1956, and may be heading for extinction.

D. The Japan Communist party (Nihon-Kyôsantô). Communist strength in Japan cannot be gauged by its numerical strength in the Diet, which declined from a high of thirty-five representatives after the January 1949 elections to its present figure of two members in the lower house and two in the upper. In terms of its discipline, its hidden external support by Russia and the international party organization, and its potential appeal in times of crisis to possible millions not now swayed by its program, the Japan Communist party must be considered one of the major parties. Its avowed aims include immediate withdrawal of United States security forces, abrogation of the United States-Japanese defense pact, continued disarmament, and social reforms. Incorporation of Japan into the Communist bloc of nations is an ultimate aim.

During the occupation years the party offered a program of so-called peaceful revolution, designed to build popular support and at the same time ward off the wrath of the occupying authorities that would have resulted from a more overtly revolutionary policy. In consequence, orders from Moscow in January 1950 purged top Japanese party officials, replacing them with others who supported more radical methods. Purge from the opposite direction in July 1950 followed the outbreak of the Korean War. The party's official newspaper, the *Akahata,* was forced to suspend publication at the same time that other measures were taken by the occupation to prevent Communist obstruction of the United Nations war effort. Since the peace treaty became effective in April 1952, the party has again enjoyed the legal status of all other parties.

Composition of the House of Representatives, by parties, as of November 1955, was as follows:

Liberal-Democratic party 299
Socialist party 154
Communist party 2
Other parties 6
Independents 3
Vacancies 3

Total 467

ULTRANATIONALISM IN POSTWAR JAPAN [5]

There have been many changes in the decade since occupation planners fashioned a democratic structure for Japan. More and more old patterns, personalities, and themes return to the stage. Premier Yoshida was succeeded by Mr. Hatoyama, the only prewar politician favored by a personal purge decree from General Mac-Arthur's headquarters. Of the seventeen members of the Hatoyama cabinet . . . eleven were under the occupation's ban, and Foreign Minister Shigemitsu served a five years' sentence as a major war criminal. The Liberal-Democratic party, a merger of the two conservative groups, commands a substantial majority in the lower house of the Diet and is committed to establishment of "public morality," educational reform, and changes in occupation laws to make them "conform with

[5] From an article by Marius B. Jansen, associate professor of Japanese history, University of Washington. *Political Quarterly*. 27:141-51. April 1956. Reprinted by permission.

national conditions." Steps are being taken to recentral-
ize the educational system, standardize textbooks, and
control their selection. And while revision of the constitutional ban on maintenance of a "war potential" is still
in preparation planes and tanks are under manufacture.

Yet it is much too early for sweeping verdicts on
the demise of Japan's new democracy. Everywhere new
interest groups which have had a decade to root themselves stand to protest and moderate the plans of the
conservatives. Education boards and teacher groups are
waging a vigorous campaign against the centralization
and standardization which is planned. The labor unions
are preparing a spring offensive to protect their gains
and secure further benefits. Constitutional revision is
still very far from accomplished. The united Socialists
lose no opportunity to challenge the less united conservatives. And there is room for misgivings about the justice
of the sweeping condemnations of occupation days. Most
of the present leaders stood against the extremism of
war-time. The reappearance of Mr. Hatoyama and Mr.
Shigemitsu does not necessarily mean a return of prewar
nationalism, and the reappearance of some of the war-
time military in posts of responsibility does not fore-
doom a rebirth of prewar militarism.

Ultranationalist Terrorist Societies

But there is no room for doubt as to the undesir-
ability of the return of ultranationalist, terrorist societies.
Such groups have gained in number and in boldness, and
their prewar leaders have regained some of the prestige
and respectability that they lost in defeat. As currents
of nationalism rise again, the ultranationalists rush to
make their old claims of national superiority. An esti-

mate of the strength and possibilities of the right-wing
organizations, of their activities and handicaps in postwar Japan, can serve as a useful indication of the distance which the Japanese people are prepared to travel
in going back to the old ways.

Rightist activities reached their postwar high during
the closing days of the Yoshida Cabinet in 1954. In that
year nationalist groups dropped leaflets from planes, they
showered leaflets on Diet sessions, they made at least
four plots against Mr. Yoshida's life, and addressed over
fifty threats to him. In November 1954 ultranationalists
staged their first public demonstration since Japan's defeat. Four thousand members and affiliates of the National Martyr Youth Corps (Junkoku Seinendan) rallied
at Hibiya Hall in Tokyo. Among the speakers was
Yoshio Kodama, a prominent prewar terrorist and war-
time navy agent, who assailed both the Yoshida government and Japanese Communists. After his speech came
a street demonstration. The Martyrs wore their dark
blue uniforms with caps and black combat boots. They
marched quietly, carrying banners inscribed with patriotic slogans, to the accompaniment of the national
anthem. This rally illustrates some of the distinctions to
be drawn when discussing the postwar right wing in
Japan. Kodama attacked both the centrist conservatives
and the left. The rally was very different from those
sponsored by leftist groups; rigid discipline and order
were marked, and not a woman was present.

The right wing in postwar Japan tries to carry on the
work of prewar ultranationalists. It recruits followers
among those who believe that Japan's war aims were
basically just and that Japan was defeated because it
failed to live up to its noble spirit. Postwar changes in
democratization represent, they feel, still another failure

to abide by that spirit, and close ties with America are unworthy of the historical mission of Japan. Renovation, purity, and self-respect will provide cures for corruption in politics, cowardice in diplomacy, and selfishness in family and society. Japan can then be saved from the dangers of the left, it will be unencumbered by the self-seeking, craven politicians, and it will be free of Mr. Dulles and the MacArthur constitution.

Although many writers use the term "fascist" when discussing Japanese ultranationalist organizations, the European exemplifications of that term fit the pre- and postwar pattern in Japan rather poorly. The main stream of the Japanese rightist movement has been rooted in the distinctive mixture of traditional and industrial values and practices in Japanese society, and its works can be understood only by considering the tensions on which it has fed.

The right-wing organizations of twentieth-century Japan trace their ancestry back to societies formed by disgruntled ex-Samurai in the early years of the 1880's. Their founders were alarmed by the extent of social and ideological change that had followed the overthrow of the feudal regime, and they feared that Japan was leaving its proper course. They were obscurantists and xenophobes, and they were happy to receive support from segments of the business world (notably the coal industry) which valued their insistence on expansion and internal unity. The most celebrated of these organizations, the Kokuryukai (Black Dragon, or Amur, Society), formed in 1901, combined an insistence on traditional values with a call for leadership in Asia. Its members fostered study of Asian conditions and helped refugee Asian leaders, and they considered themselves self-appointed guardians of the national morality. Be-

sides receiving support from sections of the business,
army, and governmental groups, the ultranationalists
were involved in many questionable transactions on the
borderline between legitimate business and labor racket-
eering. Their organizations were not secret societies,
but neither were they mass societies. They were small
elite groups clustered around leaders who made every
attempt for full publicity in order to exaggerate their
influence. . . .

Decline of the Prewar Rightists

But the influence of the ultranationalists in prewar
days can easily be exaggerated. The rightists never
achieved unity, and they never won power. . . .

The surrender brought a sudden halt to the rightist
organizations. Although a small number of extremists
believed, with the young officers who assaulted the palace
guard, that the surrender was against the will of the
emperor, there were remarkably few spectacular protests
or suicides. Kodama reappeared briefly as councillor in
the post-surrender cabinet of Prince Higashi-Kuni, but
before long he was in Sugamo Prison while Higashi-
Kuni was operating a grocery store. General Mac-
Arthur's headquarters moved promptly against the rightist organizations, dissolving 232 and purging some 3,000
leaders from public life. Some attempted new organizations only to have them stopped by summary orders
from SCAP. But in any case the post-surrender days
contained few opportunities for rightist propaganda.
The deflation of war-time boasts of Japanism, national
essence, and national purity was climaxed when the occupation proved to be humane instead of vindictive. Kodama, who writes that he never sensed defeat despite the

bombings and horrors of the war, was crushed to find that the Americans were well-behaved. "When I first saw with my own eyes the civilized occupation," he notes, "I could not but cry out from the bottom of my heart, 'Japan has been defeated. We have been defeated!' " . . .

Reappearance of Extremists

The ultranationalist leaders have been able to resume open work since the mass depurges of the late occupation years. In 1950 the Korean War centered attention on the Communist danger, and the following year came the San Francisco Peace Treaty which brought independence in the spring of 1952. Since then the soil for a new rightist movement has been good. Social confusion, economic boom and fears of panic, a middle class hard hit by inflation, the continuing presence of foreign troops, and the constant picture of political corruption have provided potential demagogues with rich material. In 1951 . . . [it was] estimated that 540 branches of 266 organizations were in being. In July 1954 a newspaper summary counted over 700 branches with a total membership of 200,000.

Most of the organizations are related to prewar bodies, and several, like the Fatherland Protection Corps, are led by assassins of the early 1930's. Two or three such organizations may be taken as outstanding. The Fatherland Protection Corps devotes itself to fighting communism, political corruption, and giving "proper guidance to youth." It has about thirty standing members who dress in a uniform patterned on that of the American Air Force, and a total membership of around 500. Fourteen members, quartered in Tokyo for "group training" in Spartan living, devote themselves to fencing, judo, and ceremonies revering the emperor. The Martyr Youth Corps . . . was formed in 1952 by Hidezo Toyama, son of Japan's greatest prewar ultranationalist. It advocates patriotism as "the only salvation for the nation which is now contaminated by both communism and the tendency to be servile to the United States." Its Tokyo headquarters houses thirty carefully selected young men (frequenters of slot-machine parlors and romantic films are excluded) who drill and study under banners reading: "All members will die for the sake of the country."

The Seisantō (Production Party) is a revival of a group organized by the Black Dragon Society in 1931. It was originally designed as an anti-Communist group among the proletariat, but since its leader was a labor contractor and the organization was financed by Osaka business men its success was not great. The postwar Seisantō claims twenty thousand "troops" in the Osaka area, but police concede them one tenth as many. Its program calls for complete independence for Japan, including an "independent constitution," a grand union of a self-reliant Asia, and absolute peace. In 1954 the president and chairman of its central executive committee traveled to Formosa to confer with Chiang Kai-shek about the self-reliant Asia. The travelers told reporters that they conceived of national socialism as the answer to the two competing power systems of Russia and America, and that after their visit to Formosa they hoped to go to the mainland to persuade Mao to leave the Russian orbit in return for leading Japan out of the American orbit.

A Seisantō leader, Toshiharu Kawakami, also heads the League for the Defense Against Communization (Sekka boshi dan) which he formed in May 1952, after the Communist demonstrations on May Day. The League's platform features worship of the Imperial family, love of the fatherland, freedom and rights of the people, and annihilation of Communist influence. Kawakami, grandson of a xenophobic swashbuckler of [Meiji] Restoration days who slew one of Japan's great westernizers, is admirably equipped to train the 120 men he houses in his Kyoto residence. Among those receiving drill in swordsmanship, boxing, judo, and ideology is a youth who tried to assassinate Mr. Yoshida in 1954. . . .

Evaluating the Threat

From all of this it would be possible to draw very gloomy conclusions about the prospects for democracy in Japan. Nevertheless from a study of the evidence available one is led to the conclusion that the rightists have very few of the advantages that were theirs in prewar Japan while they have retained their handicaps. The reemergence of colorful terrorists of the 1930's does not mean that methods that were then effective can now succeed.

First of all, the ultranationalists have been unable to work together. . . . The ultranationalists have also failed to come up with any really new ideas. . . . The leaders cannot form mass movements, and yet it takes a mass movement to get results in postwar Japan. . . .

What can the ultranationalists promise would-be supporters? Japan's relations with Asia furnish an illustration of the way old slogans have lost efficacy. Before the war, rightist leaders could point to ties with Asia in ideological and political programs. They promised Asian reformers Japanese help, and they promised Japanese leaders Asian followers. And, failing leadership, there was always the possibility of conquest. But today conquest, even of South Korea, is unthinkable. And the rightists can hope to talk with almost no Asian leaders in ideological terms—with the possible exception of Chiang Kai-shek and Syngman Rhee, neither of whom has proven eager to follow Japanese leadership in the past. It is the left, and not the right, that can offer Japanese businessmen ties with China today.

And . . . the rightists never really won out in the 1930's. They merely provided the instability in which the military could take over. Their program, when shorn of its mysticism and Confucianism, amounted to preparing the stage for army take-over; the army, they thought, would know what to do next. But there is no comparable group with which the ultranationalists can work in the new Japan.

But once these disclaimers of imminent disaster are made it must still be granted that the ultranationalist revival presents a real danger to Japan. So long as young fanatics see in chauvinism a code of values, so long as politics are corrupt, and so long as depression lurks behind the precarious balance of imports and exports, Japan's new democracy will be vulnerable to attack by the demagogues. Economic pressures caused by rearmament can add to the difficulties and opportunities. Governmental attempts to revive patriotism and loyalty as preliminary steps to rearmament offer new dangers. And, while the old values are still in decline, no new codes have come in to inspire the idealism of the young. This is a setting in which the extremism of the left and right can thrive.

Thus the rightists are a significant sign of a partial return to prewar patterns in postwar Japan. But unless standards of national and international political and economic health dwindle rapidly the ultranationalists seem most unlikely to regain the influence that was theirs a decade and more ago. Their problems illustrate the fact that despite the apparent identity of persons and themes in postwar Japan, the total balance of forces has changed very considerably since 1945.

THE JAPANESE COMMUNIST PARTY: STRATEGY AND STRENGTH [6]

The signing of the Japanese Peace Treaty and the United States-Japan Security Treaty at San Francisco in September 1951 was the occasion for an unprecedented shift in the Communist party line on Japan. A little more than one month before Stalin's historic 1952 New Year's message to the Japanese people in which he wished them "success in their courageous struggle for independence," the Cominform (Communist Information Bureau) recast the erstwhile imperialist state in the role of colonial appendage of foreign imperialism, thereby placing Japan for the first time in history in the category of the anticolonial nations of Asia. . . .

Significantly, the "1951 Thesis," as the new party program came to be called, remained the basic policy guide for post-treaty strategy and tactics of the Japanese Communist party (JCP) at least up to the party's national council meeting in July 1955. . . .

Party Strength

According to official registration figures party membership reached a peak of 100,000 in March 1950, but it

[6] From "Japanese Communism and the Moscow-Peking Axis," article by Rodger Swearingen, associate professor of international relations, School of International Relations, University of Southern California. *Annals of the American Academy of Political and Social Science.* 308:63-75. November 1956. Reprinted by permission.

dwindled gradually to 65,000 in January 1951, 59,000 in May, 56,000 in August, and 48,000 in June 1952. Its actual strength including nonregistered members, which was once thought to be several times the registered membership, was estimated early in 1954 to be between 60,000 and 70,000. The number of members who actually pay dues to the party was at the same time said to be between 20,000 and 30,000.

A comparison of Communist results in the elections of 1949, 1952, 1953, and 1955 offers another indication of trends in post-treaty Communist strength. On October 1, 1952, a national election was held after a lapse of nearly four years. The Communists campaigned vigorously, putting up one candidate for each constituency throughout the country. Whereas thirty-five Communist candidates had been elected in the preceding election, not a single seat was won by the Communist party in the new House of Representatives. The aggregate vote declined from 2,980,000 (9.1 per cent) in the 1949 election to 890,000 (2.5 per cent) in the 1952 election. In the general election of April 19, 1953, the Communist vote decreased to 660,000 (1.89 per cent) of the total votes cast, and the party managed to win one seat in the House of Representatives. The February 1955 elections to the House of Representatives shows the first slight reversal in the downward trend in JCP popularity. Two JCP members were elected, both of them from Osaka; the party polled 773,120 (2 per cent) of the total votes cast.

JCP and the Socialists

During 1954, the Communist party continued to woo the Socialists, but the latter remained largely unconvinced of the necessity, value, or wisdom of accepting

Communist bids for "joint action." To be sure, certain
of their objectives coincided with those of the JCP, and
the Communist party "used" the Socialists when and
wherever possible.

Propaganda Themes

The principal Japanese Communist propaganda cam-
paigns of 1954-1955 revolved around themes of opposition to rearmament, military bases, and mutual security
aid, while the most sensational issue which the party
was able to exploit was the "Bikini incident," involving atomic fallout on the Japanese fishing vessel *Lucky
Dragon.*

The Labor Front

The party has been most active on the labor front,
with the 3-million-member General Council of Trade
Unions of Japan (Sohyo) an identifiable target. By
1954 Communist influence on the Council had become
substantial, but it appears to have declined somewhat
since that time. The party has made relatively less headway with the farmer and fisherman, and redoubled
efforts have recently been called for.

Sixth National Council Meeting

After the Geneva "summit" conference, the JCP
began to display aspects of the Soviet "new look." This
was in line with the world-wide Communist policy and
was not an unexpected development. Certain other related domestic developments also appear to have influenced the transformation in JCP policy, especially the
evident failure of the party's militant underground policy

and the replacement of the Yoshida government by the Hatoyama government, with the increased strength of the Socialist parties (and union as the Social Democratic party), which, in turn, tended to create what the JCP apparently regarded as a more fluid political situation.

The new modified policy was adopted at the party's sixth national council meeting in July 1955, and was published almost immediately in *Akahata*. After commenting on "favorable" developments on the international scene (such as the Geneva and the Bandung conferences) and noting that "the American imperialists are still supervising and controlling our industry, agriculture, and finances and trade, and exploiting and plundering our people," the document takes up several fundamental problems and errors, identified as failure to overcome factionalism and to unify the party, the tactical error of leftist adventurism, and the inability to strengthen the ties between the party and the people. Each of these is elaborated in some detail with the appropriate "lessons the party must learn." The document concludes by pinpointing specific target areas or groups and suggesting that there is an appropriate tactic towards each in the national-democratic liberation revolution.

The new tactical line as outlined by the Resolution, reminiscent of Mao's New Democracy, may be summarized as follows: (1) Win labor and farmers by "correcting the error of leftist sectionalism," by paying more attention to the laborer's and farmer's daily needs, by not forcing "mechanically the party's program on groups" but by "winning them ideologically." (2) "Eradicate existing prejudice in the party against intellectuals" and channel the political consciousness of the intellectuals, youth, and women toward the correct cause. (3) Correct mistakes such as supporting Shigemitsu and attacking the

Socialist party—fight for the unity of all democratic forces. (4) Be ready to exploit dissatisfaction with the Japanese government on the part of small- and medium-sized businesses, while realizing at the same time that various types of governments, though reactionary and pro-United States in large measure, can nevertheless contribute to the revolution. (5) While the party must not ally itself with monopoly capital, which supports traitors and reactionary governments, certain "dissatisfied big bourgeois" may be "encouraged" to take a neutral position. (6) Expose and block the revival of anti-Communist, Fascist, terrorist, rightist groups. (7) Organize a broad peace movement among people of all walks of life who are against atomic war—the party must, in effect, stand publicly for neutralism while not being itself neutral. (8) The party must raise its ideological level.

YOSHIDA—"DEEP BOWS AND A TEMPER" [7]

Since Yoshida emerged in 1946 from the status of a diplomat laid on the shelf by the military to that of the potentially most powerful statesman of postwar Japan, a dozen epithets, not all of them complimentary, have been applied to the man and his policies.

He has, for instance, been called a representative of the "extreme right," but this, except as a shorthand description of an old-fashioned Japanese conservative, is scarcely correct. He is profoundly anti-Communist, and suspicious of anything resembling fellow-traveling. He made some sensation when, in the early stages of his last election campaign, he angrily called Japan's Left-wing Socialists Communists or little better. He is almost

[7] From an article by Lindesay Parrott, former chief of the New York *Times* Tokyo Bureau. New York *Times Magazine*. p 12+. September 6, 1953. Reprinted by permission.

devoutly royalist, convinced, as perhaps most Japanese are, that the imperial institution, no matter to what evil uses it may have been put in the past, is the pivot around which the nation turns.

"Extreme right" in Japan has a special connotation—the return of the military caste, reestablishment of tough-muscled secret societies and "young officers" groups which dominated Japan before the war, government-backed family monopoly, and reestablishment of an aggressive empire to dominate a new Greater East Asia. None of these objectives has been endorsed by Mr. Yoshida.

The policies he has followed . . . might be described as somewhat to the right of middle of the road. They, as he has outlined them in campaign speeches, addresses to the Diet, parliamentary committee testimony and rather rare press interviews, are about as follows:

On international relations: Close alignment with the United Nations and with the United States. "Empty arguments" by the Left and the idealist intellectual fringe for absolute and unarmed neutrality in a troubled world and against "one-sided reliance on America alone" are Communist traps against which Japan must be on guard.

On rearmament: Japan must have the forces for self-defense and to insure internal security, but this requires no immediate revision of the postwar national constitution outlawing war forever. Arming of Japan, however, must wait on Japan's economic progress. "Under the present economic conditions, the construction of a single battleship would upset the whole of government finance."

On foreign aid: As the United States assisted Japan immediately after the war, so America will continue—indeed has promised—to lend a hand through special procurement. MSA [Mutual Security Administration] aid would be acceptable. The United States would be expected to make "no unreasonable demands" for an arms program that might wreck the Japanese economy.

On trade with communism: A profitable export-import relationship between Japan and China remains a question mark. Under the circumstances, Southeast Asia is Japan's most likely source of raw materials and potentially her best customer.

These are scarcely the opinions of an "extreme Rightist." If Yoshida's views require a special characterization, they smack more of the outlook of the statesmen of the Meiji era, during which, in Tokyo, he was born, than they do of anything extreme.

Yoshida was born a Takeuchi, a wealthy . . . family, identified with the politics of the early imperial revival. In common with many Japanese of every class, he bears an adopted name. His adoptive father was Kenzo Yoshida, a business man and manufacturer of silk. Yoshida passed through the Tokyo Imperial University, then an essential training ground for public servants.

From 1906 to 1939 he worked his way through the ranks of the imperial diplomatic corps, in China, in Rome and finally as ambassador to the Court of St. James—a servant of the throne and a member of the professional-business man's caste, little if at all responsible to the shifting political administrations of Japan.

It is conceivable that England, another island empire with a long royal tradition and a civil service upper class, colored Yoshida's views more than any other nation in which he served. This and his advocacy of amity with China were the main reasons for his earning the distrust of the military clique that drove Japan's government into the camps of Britain's foes in World War II. For opposing the militarists Yoshida in 1936 was vetoed as foreign minister in the new cabinet formed after key antimilitarists gained control of Japan's government. With the outbreak of the war in Europe Yoshida, then president of the Japan-Britain Society, went into virtual retirement. After Pearl Harbor he smuggled to the then interned United States Ambassador, Joseph C. Grew, his regrets over Japan's plunge into the war. He spent the last three months of the war in prison for advocating peace negotiations through British channels. . . .

It is perhaps a paradox that Yoshida, after his career as a diplomat and a retirement which he probably designed to be permanent, was tossed into the dogfight of postwar Japanese party politics more or less by accident. Originally in occupied Japan, under General Douglas MacArthur as Supreme Commander for the Allied Powers, Ichiro Hatoyama, ex-cabinet minister and politician, organized and led the conservative forces, was elected to the Diet and virtually assured of the first ministry. Then, suddenly, he was purged for his acts and writings while Japan was still a member of the Axis. Yoshida, with little or no knowledge of party politics, took the job almost by default.

The occupation ended and the purges were withdrawn. But when Hatoyama attempted to reassume control of the party he had formed Yoshida was in full command.

ICHIRO HATOYAMA [8]

The transfer of power [in December 1954] from the Liberals of ex-Premier Shigeru Yoshida to Hatoyama's Democrats was in great part a result of Hatoyama's

[8] From "Japan—Land of the Reluctant Sparrows." *Time.* 65:34-7. March 14, 1955. Reprinted by permission.

personal popularity, his canny exploitation of Japan's disillusionment with his highhanded and distant predecessor, Yoshida. But, as Hatoyama was among the first to acknowledge, his mandate went far deeper than a change of personalities. In sweeping out the Liberals, the Japanese were sweeping away a regime that represented to the majority of Japanese a decade of meek complaisance to the commands and suggestions of the United States occupiers. . . .

In place of the Yoshida men, the electorate had turned to men of almost identical pin-stripe; indeed, some were the very same men. But they wore new colors —more independence from the United States; negotiations with the Chinese Communists and Russia; some second thoughts about rearming and lining up on the Western side of the cold war. ". . . I feel that alignment only with the Western nations and the ignoring of the Communist nations . . . could lead to a third world war," said Ichiro Hatoyama. "I would like to awaken the people to a deeper, more serious sense of their independence."

A Tokyo businessman put it more crudely. "Yoshida," he said, "sold Japan from under his kimono, like a Parisian selling dirty pictures. Hatoyama is different. He is like a brand-new shopkeeper on the Ginza—his door is open to everybody." . . .

For all his political canniness and his present popularity, it is by no means certain that aged, crippled Ichiro Hatoyama is the one who can do the job. He is essentially a politician, a man who made his way up by nifty deals across the . . . [gaming] tables, by tough brawling in the Diet (once he rushed to the rostrum and tried to punch a fellow Diet member in the nose), and by tacking with the winds of national sentiment. "He is not the kind of leader who stands out and looks down on the people," said a friend, "but more the kind who leads by standing in the middle of them."

His manner and his mode of living are Western. Brought up on John Wesley and Adam Smith, he worshiped for years as a Christian, and still devotes several hours a week to robust singing of Christian hymns. But when the militarists took over in the 1930's to pursue their dream of empire, Hatoyama accepted it, endorsed it on a tour of foreign capitals, wrote a book praising Hitler and Mussolini. He was not close enough to the team to be completely trusted, so before war's end he was nudged into retirement; but he was not clean enough to pass the occupation's purview, and was purged (along with 201,815 other Japanese) after he had formed the postwar Liberal party and was about to become premier.

Until he could return, Hatoyama entrusted the Liberal party to his good friend Yoshida. By the time he was depurged five years later, Hatoyama had been laid low by a stroke, and tough-minded Shigeru Yoshida had grown too attached to the job to relinquish it. Hatoyama bided his time until the conservatives and their business backers began chafing under Yoshida's leadership, and the public began showing its irritation with the remnants of United States occupation and those who cooperated with it. All that was then necessary was a shrewd deal across the game tables. Overnight . . . a chunk of the Liberals broke off, styled themselves the Democrats, and chose Ichiro Hatoyama as their leader. Another convenient arrangement with the Yoshida-hating Socialists knocked the premier out and brought Hatoyama in.

III. JAPAN'S ECONOMIC PROBLEMS

EDITORS' INTRODUCTION

An understanding of Japan is impossible without a grasp of the problems arising from her island economy. Forced to rely for her economic existence on imports of raw materials and on export of finished goods, she has since the end of World War II struggled to stabilize a shaky balance of trade. While the country shows signs of a remarkably quick industrial recovery, she still desperately needs markets abroad to support a growing population and an expanding economy. Until recently, Japan depended almost exclusively on Western markets; now she is turning to Asia and Communist China.

The first article in this section gives a general picture of the nature of Japan's economy and the twin problems of population and labor force. An article from the New York *Times* special section on foreign trade (January 1957) shows Japan's rapid postwar industrial progress. Another article briefly describes the role of trade unions in Japanese industry and politics. The comeback of Japan's giant prewar trade combines is reported in a news story from *Newsweek*. Japanese-United States trade relations are first taken up in a discussion of the invasion of United States markets by Japanese goods. This is followed by a short news story from the New York *Times* on the boycott by southern states of Japanese textiles. An article by C. L. Sulzberger warns that Japan is being forced to look to China for markets as a result of restrictive measures taken by Western countries against Japanese goods. Another New York *Times* news story reports on the Japanese lifting an embargo on 272 items to be shipped to China. In the concluding article Vera Micheles Dean sums up Japan's economic dilemma, raising the further question of the country's new need to divert money and manpower to defense (with the withdrawal of the United States Armed Forces).

THE NATURE OF JAPAN'S ECONOMY [1]

Few travelers to Japan realize they are visiting three different but related countries. In the rice paddies farmers use methods of hand labor which date back to primitive times; in the small shops and cottage industries there are medieval-feudal patterns of manufacture and distribution, and even semifeudal social relationships; in the large factories labor unions are strong, and there are faint beginnings of automation and of an economy of abundance.

On the farms almost half of Japan's population reaches old age in the middle forties, and children are valued if only to take care of the prematurely aged. Indeed, in certain areas, large numbers of children are necessary if the family is to survive. Thanks to agricultural reforms, tenant farmers are now only a small minority, and democratic cooperative organizations have spread through the land.

Well-informed Japanese call the agricultural cooperatives one of the best of the occupation reforms and say that the Japanese bosses who at first dominated the cooperatives have gradually been replaced. Nevertheless American movie-makers recently found that to rent a Japanese farm, theoretically belonging to its farmer-owner, they had to consult a Nipponese Capone.

[1] From "Atlantic Report on the World Today—Japan." *Atlantic Monthly.* 198:17-22. August 1956. Reprinted by permission.

The small shops and cottage industries produce the handicrafts—pottery, lacquerware, silk, and damascene —for which Japan is famous. They also produce all sorts of industrial products on a sub-contract system, with some attempt at standardization, and with a remarkable ability to shift rapidly from one temporarily successful export to another. Here one can see at its most fascinating the Japanese social system of paternalism, or substitute father, substitute child, as the Japanese sociologists call it. One does not fire an inefficient father or an incapable son, but one does not need to pay him very much either.

On the farms the working day is ten hours except at the time of planting or harvest; and the pay is often as low as $10 a month. Wages in the large industries are the best in Japan, about $55 a month. Usually the working day is eight hours, and the productivity of these workers is far greater than that of workers in smaller industries.

Too Many People

The population of Japan is steadily increasing. In a country roughly the size of California (which has about 13 million inhabitants) there are close to 90 million, and each year 1.5 million new Japanese appear on the crowded scene.

Japan is one of two countries in the world (India is the other) in which systematic private and public efforts are being made to spread knowledge of birth control. Meanwhile abortion is widely used, and one estimate has it that there are each year as many abortions as births. . . .

The immediate question is what to do about the young employables who are already born and who for at least fifteen years will threaten the Japanese economy with chaos. The examples of Belgium and the Netherlands, both more densely populated than Japan, suggest that an answer can be found. Those who advocate emigration are fond of citing the fact that only 16 per cent of Japan's land is usable. But in this respect Japan is better off than North America, and far better off than the world as a whole. More can be done to reclaim land from the sea and, as one experiment has shown, to use land above 1200 feet in altitude.

Productivity and Efficiency

If Japanese productivity continues to increase at its present rate, there will be new jobs each year for perhaps 320,000 new workers. That leaves a balance each year of close to 400,000 young workers for whom new jobs must be found, for at least a decade. The only answer now in sight is a still further increase in productivity.

Productivity in Japan, however measured, is certainly above the prewar years—perhaps as much as 150 per cent of that period—a remarkable achievement when one remembers that Japan lost 40 per cent of its national wealth and 45 per cent of its territory in the Second World War. . . .

The Japanese, who in their internal affairs show a marked distaste for competition, are facing for the first time on a large scale the necessity for reaching a competitive position in international trade. Some Asian nations are reaching self-sufficiency in the light industrial goods Japan exported before the war; and others, such as Red China, are beginning to undersell the Japanese in exports of cloth, a Japanese world specialty. In heavy industrial goods and chemicals, Japan is a less efficient producer than the United Kingdom, West Germany, or the United States. . . .

The Fear of Competition

Japan's great pool of cheap and surplus labor is a disadvantage, rather than an advantage, for it leads to a lack of interest in efficiency. And Japanese workers in the largest labor union, Sohyo, have even opposed productivity. In all walks of Japanese society, raises in pay are awarded mainly according to seniority rather than merit; and generally speaking, it is more important to age than to think.

The unions object, for the most part, to time and motion studies, or even to aptitude testing for jobs. The main concern of a worker is keeping his job. A Japanese worker who seeks to better himself by transferring from one company to another is immediately suspect as disloyal. A worker expects his employer, or substitute father, to take care of him for life, and hiring a worker is closer to adoption of a child than to fitting the right worker to the right job.

Japanese industry is also weak in marketing practices, both in finding out whether there is any consumer demand for a given product, and in selling the product once it has been manufactured. Aside from neon lighting, advertising balloons, and a few sandwich men equipped with drums, umbrellas, and clackers, there is little salesmanship. A salesman is ranked with a factory worker in prestige.

Another weakness of Japanese industry, particularly the smaller industries, is the lack of adequate cost-accounting procedures. Often a company assigns an arbitrary price for its product and hopes for the best. Some companies will keep as many as three sets of books: one for themselves, one for their investors, and one for the government. . . .

Cultural Interchange

Japanese scholars and businessmen are now traveling abroad at a rate far greater than in the early days of the Meiji era, when Japan first made its effort to draw level with the Western world. Thanks to the Fulbright program, and similar but much smaller British, German, and French programs, foreign experts of all kinds are visiting Japan as never before in its history.

The most remarkable, and as yet little noticed, effort at cultural interchange is that represented by the still new Japan Productivity Center. Its efforts are being aided by an able and energetic group of Americans in the United States Overseas Operations Mission. These two agencies make it possible for teams of Japanese, usually twelve in number, from industries chosen with an eye to the long-range future of Japan, to visit the United States for six weeks of study. This program has only just begun, but its final effects may reach every circle of Japanese society. Badly needed in Japan is a business and industrial college which, free from tradition, could approach Japan's industrial productivity in a Japanese way. Such a college, properly run, could serve as an inspiration for Japanese education in general.

A period of far-reaching re-education lies ahead for the industrial and business world of Japan. . . .

It is not likely that the Japanese can make further improvements in Japanese industrial production without introducing industrial democracy and a more truly competitive pattern of life. In the long run, historians may be able to record that even more significant and lasting than the democratic influences of the occupation were the new democratic forces in Japanese business and education which appeared after the occupation was over.

JAPAN REGAINS PLACE AS INDUSTRIAL GREAT [2]

Japan is rapidly returning to the forefront among the great industrial nations. This is evidenced by humming factories, bustling offices, roaring traffic and huge, well-dressed throngs in hundreds of richly-stocked department stores of the nation.

Generally speaking, the people never have lived so well. If the average Japanese still cannot afford an automobile, it is now no impossible strain on his budget to buy a motorbike. He can afford electric lights in his house and a radio. The electric refrigerator is becoming common, and nearly 500,000 Japanese own television sets.

If an average annual income of about $230 a person seems inordinately low to an American, it is very high for a Japanese accustomed to an extremely frugal culture. It is about 4 per cent more than he made last year, more than 10 per cent above the peak years of 1934-36. "Real" wages, earnings beyond rising price levels, have increased 7.1 per cent in the last year. Wholesale prices jumped 24.5 index points, but the consumer price level has held to a reasonable 4.3. . . .

Analysts generally concede that the prospects for the future are bright. However it is never forgotten that Japan must import 20 per cent of her food and 80 per cent of her raw materials; that the population . . . con-

[2] From article by Robert Trumbull, chief of the New York *Times* Tokyo Bureau. New York *Times*. p47+. January 3, 1957. Reprinted by permission.

tinues to expand; and that the export economy, by which Japan must live, is at the mercy of economic winds in the buying countries.

Problems and Progress

Japanese exports are still little more than half the figure for the prewar peak years. Internally, economic expansion is being hampered by transportation bottlenecks and power shortages, which can be attributed, at least, in part, to shortsighted planning. The failure of urban gains in income to keep pace with the new prosperity of the farmers has an adverse political affect. And abroad, Japan faces new competitors and continuing discrimination against Japanese goods for one reason or another. . . .

However, the progress being made amazes observers who found a rather despairing picture here only two years ago.

From the utter economic prostration at the end of the war, Japan has risen to become the leader of the world in fishing, second in shipbuilding (first in number of ships built for export), third in cotton textile production, and sixth in steel output. And every month sees new postwar records in production.

A comparison of foreign trade figures for the first nine months of the calendar year 1956 with the totals for the comparable period in the previous year tells part of the story. The following table is in thousands of dollars:

	Jan.-Oct. 1955	Jan.-Oct. 1956
Imports	$1,516,300	$2,628,795
Exports	$1,582,000	$2,004,910

In the 1956 figure, the trade deficit of $623,885,000 is partly compensated by a $285,771,000 excess in "invisible" exports (United States procurement contracts and cash spending by United States servicemen and tourists) over invisible imports. . . .

As an indicator of domestic prosperity, production levels in mining and manufacturing, based on an index figure of 100 for 1950, hit 250.4 in August, 1956. Continued good rice crops, except in frost-stricken Hokkaido, enabled farmers to raise their consumption index to 132, against 100 for 1934-36. The same figure for urban workers was 127.1.

It would perhaps be misleading to dwell here on the contribution of the United States to the resurgence in Japan's economy. In the six years and eight months of Allied occupation under United States direction, a thorough revamping of the economic pattern, helped by a cash advance of $2 billion that is yet to be repaid, put the prostrate country back on its feet. As the occupation ended, Japan was enjoying the extraordinary boom caused by the Korean War.

United States Expenditures Cited

The negative effects of World War II on Japan's economy will continue to be felt for many years, entirely apart from the disintegration of her prewar overseas empire. She must pay reparations of $200 million to Burma, $550 million to the Philippines, and yet undetermined amounts to Indonesia and Vietnam — probably more than $1 billion in all. The United States is not expected to remit more than two thirds of the $2 billion rehabilitation and occupation debt.

Today, the United States contribution to Japan's expanding economy has its chief significance in the overseas procurement program which in 1956 has paid into Tokyo $188,345,000 in contracts awarded up to October this year. The visiting servicemen and others spend about another $325 million a year in various ways swelling the "invisible" exports.

Significant as this addition to the export economy is, Japanese analysts now say confidently that Japan would be able to survive if the United States contribution were withdrawn. They are less happy, however, over the implications of continuing and sometimes growing hostility to Japanese competition in United States markets, particularly in textiles.

Competition for Markets

The Japanese say they are among the best customers of the United States. In the first nine months of 1956, for example, Japan purchased $736 million in goods from the United States. Much of this is in raw cotton, a small part of which is made into cloth . . . and sent back to the United States, often to the dismay of American textile interests who find themselves being undersold by Japanese competitors.

It appears that this conflict will be resolved by negotiation. The Japanese have shown a willingness to impose voluntary quotas on shipments in delicate areas, and to police exporters who tend to such sharp practices as over-concentrating on easy selling items.

Reforms in Japanese selling methods are only one facet in a vastly changing business philosophy. . . . Where once Japan concentrated on cheap, inferior consumer goods and low-priced textiles, she is now going in for machinery and quality products. She also is tapping new markets to replace those she lost when her prewar colonies were taken away from her.

The new markets are in the underdeveloped countries of Southeast Asia. There Japan runs into heavy competition from India in the textile field, and there are indications that some day, Communist China, rapidly industrializing, may offer a challenge in consumer goods. So Japan is placing her dependence on heavy equipment and machinery, areas in which she can compete with the United States, Britain and Europe for the Asian market.

At the end of the year Japan sent a floating sample fair, showing a myriad of quality products, to all the great commercial ports of South and Southeast Asia. At the same time her agents are plentiful in many other countries, particularly Latin America of late, with sample cases bulging and order books open.

Resumption of formal diplomatic and trade relations with the Soviet Union, and rising hopes for an easing of restrictions on trade with Communist China in strategic goods, place new commercial vistas before Japanese industrialists.

The disturbances in the Middle East, and their repercussions on the trade patterns of West Europe, have been to Japan's advantage, perhaps more than temporarily. The diversion of South Asian orders to Japan with the closure of the Suez Canal was particularly significant. . . .

The rebirth of Japan as the "workshop of Asia," in a wider sense than before, has prompted one more historical readjustment now in process. . . . This is the development, hitherto unnecessary but vital now, of servicing facilities, pools of replacement parts, and other necessities for building permanent markets in major hardware.

THE JAPANESE LABOR MOVEMENT [3]

One cannot understand the present condition of Japan's labor movement and with it the nature of its social problems without at least a cursory look at the structure of the Japanese economy. Side by side with a handful of industrial giants, there are many thousands of small enterprises that are little more than artisans' shops. The larger firms, those with more than two hundred workers, employ only thirty per cent of the labor force. The big companies generally comply with the United States-inspired labor laws that were introduced after the war. In these companies the workers are organized. The smaller enterprises, employing more than two thirds of all Japanese workers, do not bother much about these laws, and their employees remain largely outside the unions. Wages, too, are substantially higher in the larger enterprises, and they are the ones that are usually cited abroad.

The smaller employer still runs his business on a patriarchal basis, combining incredible exploitation (low wages, unpaid overtime, working days up to twelve or fourteen hours) with a minimum of social benefits. In many cases he employs far too many workers, because it is contrary to the traditional social code to leave relatives or friends on the street. The jobless and underemployed in all categories are estimated at a minimum of 6 to 7 million—about 16 per cent of Japan's working population of 44 million, and almost ten times the number of unemployed officially registered in the summer of 1955. . . .

Most of the 7 million unemployed and underemployed are badly off indeed. They receive a nominal pittance or

[3] From "Japan: Between Marx and the Middle Ages," article by Lily Abegg, author and expert on Japanese affairs. *Reporter*. 14:23-6. March 8, 1956. Reprinted by permission.

no pay at all. They are undernourished and desperate. Their number is further swollen by the army of day laborers who live from hand to mouth and have no unions. Many of the large Japanese enterprises employ a high percentage of day laborers because they are much cheaper. This means that the majority of Japanese workers are not organized.

What, then, is the role of the Japanese unions: that, for instance, of the large Communist-infiltrated General Council of Trade Unions (Sohyo) with nearly 4 million members?

One can say that in Japan only the "rich" workers are organized. Next to the Sohyo, the Trade Union Congress (Zenro) with about 700,000 members plays a major role. The other unions number some 2 million members altogether.

The surprising thing is that the Sohyo derives its main support from the 1.8 million workers and employees of the government and of public enterprises. Its other 2 million are made up of industrial workers from the big companies. These are the highest-paid workers in Japan; some of them are even entitled to pensions.

Naturally, not all Sohyo members are Communist-inclined, but most of the Sohyo leaders are, and they try to make their influence felt more and more. Sohyo is more a political organization than an ordinary union. In a certain sense it carries more weight than the newly reunited Socialist party of Japan with its eleven million votes.

Sohyo leadership is less concerned with the workers' welfare than with their political indoctrination. Sohyo strikes are almost always political, and pay increases and other such demands serve merely as adjuncts. Since Sohyo is mostly interested in political power, its first

interest was in the "rich" workers in the largest enterprises and the government services who could be organized more easily.

Zenro, the more moderate federation, rejects political
strikes, stresses the unions' economic tasks and is close
to the right-wing Socialists.

Recently, however, Sohyo has realized that even the
"rich" workers, the left-wing intellectuals, the frustrated
youth, and other dissatisfied groups do not add up to
enough votes for the left-wing parties. The Japanese
House of Representatives still consists of about two
thirds conservatives and one third Socialists. (The Communists have only two seats.)

For this reason, Sohyo [has] embarked . . . on a
major organizing campaign among the smaller enterprises and the day laborers. The question who will
win these unorganized masses is of major importance
for Japan.

THE COMEBACK OF THE GIANT TRADE COMBINES [4]

Prewar Japan boasted some of the biggest of the
world's big businesses. These great combines, such as
Mitsui, Mitsubishi, and Sumitomo, were broken up during the postwar occupation. Now as Japan faces an
economic crisis, they are being reformed. The following report explains the vital role these giant concerns
have played in the Japanese economy and in world trade
and outlines their plans for resuming this role. . . .

The Zaibatsu

The history of Mitsui, Mitsubishi, and Sumitomo,
the most famous of the Zaibatsu [Wealth-Clique] goes
back centuries and decades:

[4] From "Comeback of the Great Japan Trade Combines." *Newsweek*. 43:60-1.
April 12, 1954. Reprinted by permission.

Three centuries ago a family named Mitsui owned a plant making sake [the most popular alcoholic beverage of Japan, fermented from rice]. They branched out into retailing and money-lending. As Japan's industrial and commercial expansion began in the second half of the nineteenth century, Mitsui-Gumi (House of Mitsui) became in 1871 financial agent for the government, in 1872 the backers (unwillingly) of the First National Bank, and in 1876 the founders (willingly) of the Mitsui Bank.

In the days when Japan was opening up after Commodore Perry's visit, the financial adviser to the Lord of Tosa, a noble on the island of Shikoku, was named Iwasaki. He formed an enterprise called Tosa Kaisei Shosa which acquired interests in mining, manufacturing, and shipping, and became Mitsubishi.

In the sixteenth century a family named Sumitomo operated a copper refinery in Sakai. About a century later it acquired the renowned Besshi copper mines. Gradually the House of Sumitomo expanded, always with mining as its base.

In this manner the Zaibatsu rose from humble beginnings to giants that straddled the world. In late nineteenth- and early twentieth-century Japan their growth was natural against a background of rapid modernization, a growing labor supply, a shortage of capital, a small investing class, and a primitive economy.

Strict "house rules," usually laid down through the will of the founder, determined every action of the members of the Zaibatsu families although later the companies tended to supplant family rule with a paid managerial class. The firms were holding-company pyramids, each with a parent company, the Honsha, on top in control of a number of manufacturing, commercial and financial companies which in turn dominated affiliates and subsidiaries.

After the war the United States occupation began a veritable crusade aimed at tearing down these immense enterprises and "purging" practically all their executives. By 1947 these extreme measures, in the opinion of responsible officials in the Truman Administration, were threatening permanently to cripple the Japanese economy. From that time on measures were taken by Washington to temper and often to reverse the directives issued by occupation authorities. Behind the scenes the Zaibatsu companies maintained the old ties and, by the time the Japanese peace treaty was signed in 1951, it became obvious that the parent organizations would be revived in one form or another.

The old Zaibatsu had their faults. The rivalry of Mitsui and Mitsubishi through the political parties they controlled or tried to control was unhealthy. Competition to a considerable extent was stifled. The maze of interlocking companies made accurate cost accounting difficult and preserved inefficient enterprises. Nevertheless, the old Zaibatsu played a predominant role in Japan's rise to industrial greatness. Few authorities now doubt that the new Zaibatsu will have to play the same role if Japan's industrial strength is to be restored.

New Circumstances

Just as a peculiar set of economic circumstances fostered the growth of the old Zaibatsu, so postwar considerations are dictating the reappearance of the Zaibatsu in a new guise. These considerations are:

1. The general obsolescence of the Japanese industrial plant. . . . A good start has been made on the installation of new machinery but there is still a long road ahead before Japan can measure up to such advanced countries as the United States and West Germany.

2. The need for large industrial facilities to cope with rearmament orders.

3. A high wage structure for Japan and a great need for "rationalization" in the employment of labor.

4. The high price of imported raw materials. Japan lost control of important raw-material areas in the war. The postwar period, generally speaking, has brought greater rises in raw-material prices than in those of manufactured products—to Japan's detriment.

5. Tough competition in the regions that are natural markets for Japanese products. The Germans, notably, are underselling the Japanese in Southeast Asia, India, and the Middle East.

6. The closing off of some natural markets, such as China, and the difficulty of developing trade in other natural markets, such as the Philippines, because of political considerations.

Toward the Future

In order to cope with these circumstances, the Japanese need companies with large reserves of capital, good credit ratings abroad, managerial competence, long experience in foreign markets, and a reputation for honest dealing and sound products. The reconstituted Zaibatsu firms can meet these requirements. That is the reason they are now able to go ahead with ambitious plans for the future as outlined in this report from Compton Pakenham, chief of *Newsweek's* Tokyo bureau:

The re-amalgamation of the big firms is being carried out through the banks — the Mitsubishi, Mitsui, and Sumitomo banks have dropped their occupation-imposed names—by means of stockholdings in, and loans to, previously affiliated companies. The Korean-War boom, which brought unexpected dollar orders to Japan, started this development.

For example, the Mitsubishi Bank has given priority to loans to such firms as Mitsubishi Heavy Industries, Mitsubishi Steel, and Mitsubishi Petroleum. These companies are still among the most prominent of their kind from the point of view of facilities and personnel. Other former Zaibatsu banks have followed suit, assuming more and more the aspects of holding companies along the old lines.

As such they began sending their personnel into executive positions with the firms borrowing from them. The managing director of the Mitsui Shipping Company was transplanted from the Mitsui Bank. The Mitsubishi Bank has placed directors on the boards of three former Mitsubishi Heavy Industries companies. Today all eleven of the largest shipbuilding companies have one or more bank executives on their boards.

On December 10, 1953, it was announced that four ex-Mitsubishi trading firms, Mitsubishi Shoji, Fuji Shoji, Tozai Koeki, and Tokyo Boeki, had signed an agreement to merge into a single unit under the same name as the old trading pivot of the complex-Mitsubishi Shoji (literally Commercial Affairs). Its first overseas venture will be an office, under United States law, in New York. Along the same lines, Mitsui is reorganizing the Muromachi Bussan Kaisha into a new Mitsui Bussan Kaisha (its great prewar trading unit).

The big companies, as they reorganize, are naturally playing a leading role in various schemes for increasing Japan's exports. For example, they are behind the government's plan to conclude the technical agreements with the Southeast Asian countries and the formation of an "Asia Association" for trade promotion.

MADE IN JAPAN [5]

More and more United States stores, especially in the East and on the West Coast, are carrying Japanese goods —toys, cameras, chinaware, sewing machines, furniture, ladies' blouses, cashmere sweaters, silks, Christmas ornaments, pearls. Add these items to heavy imports of plywood, tuna, and cotton cloth and you have a real movement into the United States market. . . . Japanese traders, sometimes aided by United States importers, have shown a remarkable ability to find a whole new gamut of products for the United States market. On top of that they have had official United States help in reestablishing Japan's traditional markets in this country. This has been part of our Pacific strategy aimed at hanging on to our principal ally in the area and helping it become economically strong again.

Success in the American Market

Some United States industries feel that the tariff concessions carry this help beyond reasonable bounds. They recall that in the 1930's some United States industries were pushed to the wall by cut-throat Japanese competition based on "starvation" wages and "dumping." Even if these practices are not revived, Japanese success in the United States market has already given quite a few businessmen cause for worry.

In Japan, interest in the United States market has reached fever pitch. Fred H. Schoeman, vice president for the Far East of Metasco, Inc., importing subsidiary of Allied Stores Corp., says hardly a week goes by that a Japanese manufacturer doesn't drop by his New York

[5] From "Made-in-Japan: A New Record." *Business Week.* p 148+. September 24, 1955. Reprinted by permission.

office asking for advice about tackling the United States market. Other importers tell of receiving direct-mail advertising from Japan. And the Japanese government's trade and information center on Fifth Avenue in New York is sparking all kinds of promotional gimmicks. . . .

This enthusiasm for making a big pitch at the United States market is paying off. Metasco, for example, has developed a whole line of modern design dinnerware manufactured from basic Japanese patterns. The quality of the article does not recall cheap Japanese imports of the past. Metasco is using snob-appeal to sell the merchandise, including promotions with Shirley Yamaguchi, Japanese movie star now in United States films.

Japan's blossoming postwar optical industry with its 35mm. cameras, binoculars, and microscopes is another example of new products in the United States market. Japan is selling cashmere sweaters, in direct competition with Britain; they have almost become a staple in many West Coast department stores and are seen increasingly in the East. Some scientific instruments of high quality and low price — a voltameter, for example — are now entering the United States market. Most retailers report that the high quality of these new Japanese products is overcoming whatever sales resistance there might have been in the past to Japanese imports.

The Japanese, in fact, are moving into higher priced goods as a planned policy. And it isn't just a tactic to defeat United States protectionist interests. They recognize that merely copying United States and European products and selling them for a lower price won't gain the ends of the Japanese export program. Japan must put as much labor as possible into the exports it makes from raw material imports. The Japanese feel that's the only way their industry can support the country's growing population.

Most United States importers agree with this policy. "The only way we can help ourselves and the Japanese is to raise the level of the quality of Japanese imports into this country," Schoeman of Metasco says. He also acknowledges that higher quality and prices for an imported article mean larger profits for the importer. Schoeman believes a whole new group of Japanese products, based on Japan's great artistic traditions, can change United States homes as much as the Scandinavian-modern designs did in the 1930's and the 1940's.

American Resistance

But not all United States importers are willing to go along with this appeal to higher quality and higher priced merchandise. That's why there have been several powerful, if little publicized, blowups in Japanese imports. . . .

In cotton textiles, the Japanese are trying a . . . policing system. The Japanese Cotton, Yarn, & Cloth Export Association . . . [has] provisionally decided to curtail all exports to the United States and Canada, and made plans to set up minimum quality standards for United States shipments.

A part of this story is the "notorious dollar blouse," as one Japanese consular official in New York calls it. Two Japanese companies, after three years of study in the United States market, began turning out a blouse that could be sold here for $1 or even 89 cents. So far more than 1 million have been ordered in Japan. Now the Japanese government has moved in and put a floor under blouse prices. Last year a similar situation occurred with sewing machine heads. . . . The present Japanese government has been quick, in most cases, to act in response to American industries' demands. It knows that sharp tactics by Japanese traders could undermine the whole United States-Japanese alliance.

So far, by working with United States importers and trade associations, this policing has been successful. It remains to be seen whether it will be equally effective as the volume of Japanese imports rises. If it is not, outcries from United States industry and protectionist forces in Congress are likely to bring quotas on Japanese imports.

The reduction of some tariffs . . . has sharpened the demands of some United States manufacturing firms for such quotas. Thomas N. Ingram, head of the Charlotte, North Carolina, branch of the American Cotton Manufacturers Institute, asserts that quotas will be necessary in his industry.

But the cotton textile problem is not simply one of undercutting domestic production by Japanese cheap labor—receiving sometimes as little as a tenth of United States wages. Japan's textiles were almost completely destroyed by the war. Facilities have now been rebuilt in the most modern fashion, and as a result productivity is up 15 per cent to 20 per cent. That's why, in spite of substantial wage increases, Japanese textiles are cheap.

This agitation by the textile industry has been intensified by the tariff concessions. There's a feeling that the concessions will make the greatest difference in the United States textile industry. . . .

Effect on Japanese Trade

More important than any of the actual reductions in tariff, most United States observers believe, is the psychological effect on Japanese traders. The United States concessions are being taken in Japan as proof that the Administration means to back up the pledges to help Japan's comeback in world trade, which it made at . . . [the 1955] Geneva meetings on the General Agreement on Trade and Tariffs. . . .

Shikichi Minami, director of Daiichi Bussan Kaisha, Ltd., in New York, Japan's largest trading company, puts Japan's argument in a nutshell: "I hope the United States public appreciates that we must sell if we are to buy here." Japanese imports from the United States were $725 million last year [1954]—about three times Japan's sales in the United States. Furthermore, Japan bought $185 million worth of fibers, the largest single customer abroad for American cotton. Minami points out that a relatively small part of that came back as Japanese textiles—only 1.5 per cent of United States consumption.

SOUTHERN BOYCOTT OF JAPANESE TEXTILES [6]

The Administration is worried about the long-range effects of a southern campaign to boycott Japanese textiles.

The State Department has not yet spoken out or intervened lest it strengthen the forces in Congress intent on curbing the President's treaty-making powers.

On March 8 [1956] South Carolina took the lead by decreeing that wholesalers and retailers selling Japanese textiles, or garments made from them, must post a sign saying, "Japanese textiles sold here." The sign must be displayed "in a conspicuous place upon the door" in letters "not less than four inches high," the law said.

Meanwhile, the City Council of Greenwood, South Carolina, adopted a resolution March 16 urging a citizens' boycott of Japanese goods.

Alabama's legislature passed a similar bill. . . .

[6] From "Boycott of Japan Upsets Officials," by Elie Abel, New York *Times* Washington Bureau. New York *Times.* p 12. April 12, 1956. Reprinted by permission.

Tokyo protested in a note delivered . . . [in Washington]. It said the South Carolina law violated the 1953 treaty of friendship, commerce and navigation. Article 16 of the treaty accords to Japanese goods in the United States market treatment no less favorable than that received by exports from any other country.

The effect on the United States foreign policy is held damaging in these respects:

1. Discriminatory legislation of the type adopted in South Carolina contradicts the basic tenet of postwar policy for the Far East, which is to help a friendly and politically reliable Japan establish a sound economic system.

2. The boycott movement is expected to incite neutralist and left-wing politicians in Japan to step up their attacks on the United States.

3. Officials are concerned lest South Carolina's action expose United States business interests in Japan to retaliation and cause other countries to doubt similar treaties with the United States.

4. Japan is the largest single market for United States raw cotton in a period of declining exports and increasing surpluses. In 1955, the Japanese bought 647,000 bales, 26 per cent of the total exported. If Japan's textile exports encounter discrimination in the United States she may reduce raw cotton imports in retaliation.

Officials make the additional point that the United States sells far more cotton cloth to Japan than it buys in return. In the last year Japan bought 542 million square yards of cotton cloth from the United States, while exporting 99.5 million square yards.

The State Department has avoided such open intervention as urging . . . [a governor] to veto . . . [a]
bill. Secretary of State Dulles, asked about the Japanese
protest at his April 3 news conference, acknowledged
that "there is a possibility of setting up forces here which
could be very inimical to the operation of our most-
favored-nation policy with respect to trade."

THE LURE OF PEIPING [7]

Our State Department is often referred to as Foggy
Bottom because of its miasmal Potomac lowland site.
Japan's Foreign Office is similarly known as Misty Bar-
rier. Sometimes these labels stimulate sardonic quips. But
economic rather than diplomatic vapors most threaten
the health of our relations. When Wall Street sneezes,
Tokyo catches influenza.

Japan is not only our most important Asian ally but
also our second greatest international market. Commerce with us is even more vital to this land of traders.
Its diplomacy must ultimately respond to their requirements. . . .

Hopes and Prospects

The Japanese hope to expand sales in America.
Nevertheless, prospects are limited. Our manufacturers
resent the prospect of further competitive incursions.
Therefore, Tokyo scans the rest of the world for other
opportunities. However, in Western Europe it sees a
restrictive common market — sponsored by us. And in
the Commonwealth not only Britain but Australia, New
Zealand and even India refuse to accord this nation equal
treatment. In Asia, Japan is hampered by two factors.

[7] From "Can Asian Flu Come From America?" by C. L. Sulzberger, columnist for the New York *Times.* New York *Times.* p26. October 14, 1957.
Reprinted by permission.

There is a legacy of resentment left in lands like Indonesia and the Philippines by Tokyo's imperial armies. And on the mainland we have forced them to participate in our economic blockade against the Communist bloc.

While still patient under these circumstances, it is to the mainland and above all to China that Japanese industrialists ultimately look. We tell them this is a different China; that it makes its own textiles and needs its own iron and coal. But not only do the Japanese remember prewar days when Manchuria fed their hungry furnaces. Their businessmen have been scouring the continent and come back with optimistic views. This is reflected in Tokyo's diplomacy.

Japan would like to tidy up the complex Chinese picture. It favors a "two China" solution which would guarantee Formosan independence while recognizing Peiping. It hopes mercantile restrictions on the Communist bloc will gradually wither away. It even desires a reunited neutralized Korea.

These concepts run counter to some of our announced policies. As yet there is no conflict because Japanese-American trade still flourishes. The present government remains highly responsive to Washington's suggestions and politically well entrenched.

Effects on Japanese-American Relationships

But diplomacy must plan for possible contingencies. Peiping has promised massive trade if the country denounces its security treaty with us. China pledges aid in restoring sovereignty over American-occupied Okinawa. This impresses Japan's opposition Socialists. Right now they are weak and their prospects poor. But any economic crisis might easily catapult them into office. . . .

As long as we can keep . . . [Japan's] trade balances relatively healthy it is almost certain that a strongly pro-American administration will remain in office. . . . In such an event subsidiary disputes are unlikely to upset our basic position.

However, diplomacy cannot control the economics of democracy. Any recession in the United States will be mirrored in Japanese ballot boxes. Tokyo's policy, as we know better than anyone, is subject to swift and astonishing change. In Washington the Pentagon has a large say in relationships with Japan. . . . [In Japan] the big voice is business; business is survival.

EMBARGO ON TRADE WITH CHINA LIFTED [8]

Japan joined Britain and some Western European nations today in the race for the Chinese Communist market.

The Ministry of Trade and Industry announced, after a two-hour Cabinet session, a list of 272 previously banned items whose shipments to the Chinese mainland now would be permitted.

The list followed exactly the one announced . . . by Britain when she eased her trade restrictions with Communist China [in May 1957].

The changes mean that the Peiping regime will be in the same category as the Soviet Union and the Eastern European Communist countries as far as trade is concerned. Previously, some items banned for shipment to Communist China could be sent to the Soviet Union and other Communist lands.

[8] From "Japan Joins Race for China Trade," news story by Foster Hailey, Tokyo Bureau of the New York *Times*. New York *Times*. p3. July 17, 1957. Reprinted by permission.

Still restricted to all Communist countries are about 170 items, including those considered to have direct war-making potential.

The new move will be popular among members of the ruling Liberal-Democratic party as it robs the opposition Socialists of one of their main platform planks.

But Japanese trading circles expressed skepticism whether the action would mean much economically. They said that most of the items on the list were machinery and that Japanese machinery was not competitive in price with that of the British and Western European manufacturers.

The only way in which the China trade could be substantially improved, they said, would be by the extension of long-term credits. There was no indication from any government source that such a move was in prospect.

Some optimists predicted, however, that even with the handicaps of high prices and lack of official relations with the Chinese Communists, trade next year probably could be doubled from the 1956 total of $150 million.

Japan's decision to follow Britain's lead in canceling part of the United States-sponsored embargo list came as a surprise.

On his recent visit to the United States, Premier Nobusuke Kishi had left the impression in both public and private talks that Japan intended to move slowly in amending the embargo, out of deference to Washington's ideas. The Japanese press had so interpreted his words and had him for taking that attitude.

Apparently the pressure of events was so great that the Premier felt it necessary to take action promptly. Japan's trade balance has been steadily deteriorating in recent months and stringent import controls have had to be imposed. Even a small increase in exports would be heartening.

It could not be learned today whether the government intended to take any further steps to stimulate the China trade. An unofficial trade agreement expired in May and has not been renewed.

The Chinese have refused to send a trade mission to Japan unless Japan waives her requirement for finger-printing its members. The Foreign Office restated today its position that it would not grant privileges to the Chinese Communists that were not extended to other foreigners, since such a move might be accepted abroad as tacit diplomatic recognition of the Peiping Government. Japan does not appear ready to give even an appearance of inclining in that direction as yet.

THE HARD ECONOMIC FACTS [9]

Put in the bluntest terms, Japan once again faces the dilemma which harassed its pre-World War II leaders and finally induced them to embark on an attempt to conquer mainland China and Southeast Asia. Their dilemma is starkly clear. Japan, pinned into a cluster of islands which lack the principal raw materials essential for modern industry and having developed a highly industrialized economy, must import raw materials. To do this it must find expanding markets where it can sell its manufactured goods, preferably for hard currencies, American and Canadian dollars and pounds sterling.

This raw-materials-plus-export-markets dilemma had been temporarily relieved by the United States military and defense-support expenditures in Japan, first during the occupation and then during the Korean war, when Japan served as a supply base for United Nations troops.

[9] From "Japan's Year of Decisions," by Vera Micheles Dean, editor, *Foreign Policy Bulletin. Foreign Policy Bulletin.* 36:172+. August 1, 1957. Reprinted by permission.

American expenditures, in any case nonrenewable (unless war is resumed in Korea, which the Japanese are the last to wish for), will be further reduced now that the United States plans to withdraw some 25,000 ground combat troops and has transferred the Far Eastern Command from Tokyo to Hawaii. Troop withdrawal alone, it is estimated, will reduce spending by American military personnel by $100 million.

The United States plans to cushion the impact of this change-over by increasing military procurement in Japan of items needed to provide military assistance and economic aid to Asian nations. This, however, cannot of itself provide a long-term alleviation of Japan's economic problem, which is now clearly seen as a widening gap between its expenditures on imports—notably raw materials and capital goods for industrial expansion—and receipts on its exports.

The man in the street is still unaware of this problem and looks forward to the continuance of the current high employment and boom prosperity. Even government officials have been slow to recognize the possible consequences of the country's economic difficulties. At first, former Finance Minister Hayato Ikeda thought that financial controls would be sufficient to deal with the crisis. But the governor of the Central Bank, Masamichi Yamagiwa, and a five-man brain trust of economic experts appointed by Prime Minister Nobusuke Kishi urged a stern over-all plan to check the deterioration of Japan's international monetary position. . . .

New Economic Policy

The cabinet on June 14 [1957] approved a series of over-all economic measures drafted earlier by the ruling Liberal-Democratic party. These measures include inten-

sive export promotion, such as the famed export finance
system to increase exports; curbing of imports; wide
retrenchment of state investment and loan programs;
deferment of investment in plants which are not key
industries and even in some key industries; tighter controls on financial policy, accompanied by efforts to help
small industries; price stabilization; and new foreign
credits, including a loan of $125 million from the Inter-
national Monetary Fund and projected borrowing from
the World Bank and the Export-Import Bank of the
United States.

Japan's predicament is that any economic move it
makes threatens to create new problems. Cuts in government spending—particularly on housing, of which, with
the growth of population, there is a dire shortage—will
lower living standards. Emphasis on large-scale production for export may drive small enterprises manufacturing for internal consumption to the wall, creating
unemployment. In turn, unemployment would weaken
the position of the Liberal-Democratic party and play
into the hands of the opposition party, the Socialists.
And efforts to push Japanese exports invariably arouse
hostility in hard-currency countries, notably Britain and
the United States.

Trade with Asian Countries

The hard economic facts are that even with the best
will in the world, Britain, the Commonwealth and the
United States cannot provide the markets Japan needs
for its exports, if for no other reason than that they
produce much the same goods, often better, even though
sometimes more expensively. Recognizing this, Mr.
Kishi has proposed the establishment of a South Asia
Development Fund, chiefly with United States financial

contributions, under which Japan would supply manufactured goods of all kinds to the industrially less developed countries of Southeast Asia, obtaining from them the raw materials it needs.

So far, the Asian response to this proposal can only be described as cool. Except for Thailand, which escaped Japanese conquest in World War II, most of the countries of this area suffered from Japanese invasion and deprivation, and are not roused by visions of a plan which reminds them of Tokyo's wartime slogan for a "Co-prosperity Sphere." Moreover, these countries, notably the Philippines and Indonesia, demand reparations in kind from Japan. None of them wants to see Japan acting as a sort of major-domo for Washington, and all prefer to get aid from the United States direct, to be spent as they think best for their own needs. They also fear that Japan's proposal would prevent their industrialization.

The prospect for the fund, then, is distinctly dim. Japan hopes to enlist the support of India, which has already benefited by Japanese experience in rice growing and the development of small industries. Meanwhile, they talk of trade with Communist China, although they recognize that the Chinese, now engaged in an industrialization program of their own, may be unable to export much in the way of the raw materials Japan needs. What the Japanese hope for is to participate jointly with the Chinese in developing new raw materials.

But in one way or another Japan has to solve its raw-materials-plus-exports dilemma if it is to maintain its high living standard and avoid social unrest and political strains. Twenty years later, with 20 million people more, Japan faces the same problems it did before it turned to war and conquest in the early 1930's. War proved an ineffective instrument of economic policy; now Japan, with the aid of the United States and the United Nations, hopes to find a peaceful way out of its difficulties.

IV. JAPAN BETWEEN EAST AND WEST

EDITORS' INTRODUCTION

The dilemma of Japan today is most manifest in her foreign relations, which are closely interwoven with her trade relations. First, Japan's course is naturally affected by the buffetings of the cold war. Newly freed from United States military occupation, she is yet dependent on the United States for her defense. Aligned with the West, and having roundly rejected communism at home, she is nonetheless drawn to Communist China by historic ties and the need for China markets. Finally, she must reckon at home with a rising tide of pacifist, neutralist sentiment.

There are essentially three main courses open to Japan: She can remain linked with the West as a sort of junior partner of the United States; she can adopt neutrality and join with the Bandung powers as part of an Asian-African "Third Force"; or she can look for closer economic and political ties with Communist China and with the Soviet Union. At the moment it would appear that she has chosen the role of a neutral nation.

In the first article in this section Harold S. Quigley defines Japan's present neutralism. Next, Foreign Minister Fujiyama explains why it is natural for Japan to want ties with Asia. Secretary of State John Foster Dulles outlines United States policy toward Japan in terms of markets and trade. An article by Ralph Braibanti presents reasons why Japan should continue close, friendly relations with the United States. Demaree Bess reports on anti-Americanism in Japan—which was particularly rife immediately following the end of the American occupation in 1952 and now appears to be receding. Resentment continues, however, in connection with hydrogen bomb tests, a problem explored by Herbert Passin, and possession of islands claimed by Japan, the subject of two articles by Robert Trumbull. A New York *Times* news story discusses the United States stand on the Girard case and gives the facts of the incident prior to the trial and Girard's three-year suspended sentence. Another *Times* news story reports the United States-Japanese agreement to remove United States troops from Japan. The text of a Socialist resolution on foreign policy is given as of possible interest in the future in the event the Socialists take power. An article by C. L. Sulzberger takes up the thorny problem of the role of Japan in our defense planning. An article on Japanese relations with Communist China describes the ancient bonds between these two countries. The concluding article, by Edwin O. Reischauer, is a warning that the United States must do more to develop Japan's potential if we are to keep communism from sweeping Asia.

JAPAN BETWEEN TWO WORLDS [1]

The Japanese people today find themselves forced to chart a course between two opposing ideologies, neither of them indigenous to Japan. These ideologies—democracy and communism—are the roots of foreign policy in the United States and the Soviet Union. Whether or not they can find a basis for co-existence in peace is the supreme question in contemporary international relations. If they cannot, it must be expected that China

[1] From an article by Harold S. Quigley, professor of political science at the University of Minnesota and co-author of *The New Japan: Government and Politics*. *Far Eastern Survey*. 25:168-74. November 1956. Reprinted by permission.

will throw her major force on the side of the U.S.S.R. Japan lies at the doorstep of overwhelming power at a time when she has barely begun to rearm and to regain her industrial strength. That fact, in the minds of the Japanese, counsels harmony with the Communist states. On the other hand Japan needs capital and trade and the raw materials of the United States, the British Commonwealth, and Southeast Asia. It is out of these considerations that the so-called neutralism of Japan has developed.

As applied to a national attitude in time of peace this term is metaphorical rather than technically accurate. "Neutrality" is the position of a country which is nonpartisan in time of war. Historically, a weak state often has played one strong power or alliance against another, in that way maintaining its independence. The Japanese are not by nature pacifist, although they vented their belligerency in feudal rather than foreign wars for many centuries. Today they prefer to be nonpartisan because they have tasted the bitter tea of defeat and occupation. To suppose that this means that they are friendly to communism or indifferent to democracy is to misread the implications of their attitude. They want an opportunity to rebuild, to discover new means of survival, to find themselves.

Japan today is therefore bending every effort to reconciliation with the peoples of Asia and to her own rehabilitation. Her leaders are willing to pay a good price in reparation for the damage wrought in China and Southeast Asia by Japanese military action. They are hoping, partly through cultural interchanges, to redeem their country in the eyes of the youth of Asia. Japanese technicians are finding a wide market for their talents in other Asian lands. At long last the true meaning of cooperation has dawned upon the Japanese. Having learned it the hard way they are determined to experiment with it. They are making encouraging headway. Among the lesser states of East Asia whose good will has been sought, only South Korea has stood aloof. . . .

Relationship with the United States

It is apparent from recent utterances of Japanese political leaders that, while they wish to cooperate closely with the United States, they prefer to do so from a position of complete independence. Obviously they do not occupy that position at present and will not do so during the life of the existing Mutual Security Treaty and its accompanying Administrative Agreement. [Former] Prime Minister Hatoyama, who heads the majority Liberal-Democratic party, declared nearly two years ago that "national pride does not allow the indefinite continuation of a situation in which national defense is mainly dependent upon foreign military forces." The platform of his party, announced on January 1, 1956, called for development of self-defense "so as to prepare for the eventual withdrawal of foreign troops stationed in this country." Shortly before this announcement the strong, labor-backed Socialist party asserted in its platform that "Japan, since her defeat, has been seriously limited and controlled by a foreign power and is virtually in a state where she has lost her real independence." All of these statements are moderately phrased and hardly express the degree of disagreement with American policies which is felt by many Japanese. As seen by Arata Sugihara, a recognized expert on Far Eastern questions, "cooperation between the two nations should constitute the mainstay of Japan's foreign policy but

without any semi-occupational coloring." American consciousness of the absence of any thought of limiting the
independence of Japan should not lead us to discount
Japanese interpretations of our relationship to their
country. It will hardly be denied that this relationship
is of our choosing. If the Japanese do not regard it as
protective to them, its importance for the protection of
the United States will decline. If, as seems probable, its
value to both Japan and the United States can be assured
by some modification of the existing relationship that
takes fuller account of Japanese sensibilities, all relevant
factors, historical and contemporary, should be under
consideration in Washington and Tokyo to that end.

Japan and the Communist Countries

Until October 1956 the technical state of war between
Japan and the Soviet Union had continued, in view of
the latter's failure to sign the peace treaty of San Francisco. Both states desired to resume diplomatic relations
and they had been discussing possible bases of agreement
at intervals since June 1955. Speaking in the Diet on
April 25, 1955, Prime Minister Hatoyama said:

The Government, as has been stated frequently, hopes
to terminate speedily the state of war and restore normal
diplomatic relations with the U.S.S.R. The Government also
intends to make efforts to improve the trade relations between Japan and Communist China. I should like to make
clear again one particular point on this occasion. That is, the
normalization of diplomatic relations with Communist countries is one thing and the acceptance of communism is another. We are firmly resolved to adhere to our attitude of
anti-communism and to adopt every available means in defense of the cause of democracy.

He continued:

Meanwhile it is an undeniable fact that, however strongly
opposed we may be to the Communist ideology, there now

exist in the world certain powers which are adherents of communism. In dealing with such powers it would be advisable to respect each other's sovereignty and thereby to open normal diplomatic or economic relations to mutual advantage without propagandizing or trying to impose one's ideology on the other. I am firmly convinced that this very course should be adopted also as a means of forestalling another world war, the possibility of which is now filling all the peoples of the world with terror.

On February 27 of the same year the two wings of the Socialist party issued a joint statement of similar tenor. It called for the

issuance of a joint statement declaring the termination of a state of war between Japan on one side and Communist China and Soviet Russia on the other, thereby to conclude a peace treaty, to restore normal diplomatic relations, and to promote greater trade with the aforementioned nations.

Although Russia initiated an exchange of notes on January 25, 1955, indicating her readiness to negotiate in Tokyo or Moscow, and subsequently appeared to acquiesce in Japan's preference for New York, the two governments ultimately agreed upon London as the site for talks, which began on June 1, 1955. Matsumoto Shunichi represented Japan and Jacob Malik, Russia. Until March 1956 the two men sought to reach agreement on points deemed to be obstacles to the establishment of regular diplomatic relations. The principal issues arose from the diplomatic and military consequences of World War II. They involved the repatriation of Japanese held as war prisoners by Russia, Japanese claims to South Sakhalin and the Kurile Islands (all of which were Japanese before the war but are now occupied by the U.S.S.R.), and Japan's desire to resume fishing rights in Soviet-controlled waters. Also of great

importance to Japan was the vote of Russia in support
of her admission to the United Nations. When the talks
began, Japan contended that some 1,450 of her citizens
were known to be alive under Soviet detention and that
some 19,700 others had not been reported upon. . . .

Russo-Japanese Declaration

On October 19 [1956] at Moscow Bulganin and
Hatoyama signed a joint declaration which embodied
the following terms: (1) the state of war ends on the
day the present declaration enters into force; (2) diplomatic and consular relations are re-established; (3) relations will be guided by the principles of the United
Nations Charter; (4) the U.S.S.R. will support Japan's
admission to the United Nations; (5) all Japanese prisoners will be repatriated and the U.S.S.R. will investi-
gate as to the fate of other Japanese believed by Japan
to be in the U.S.S.R.; (6) the U.S.S.R. renounces all
reparations claims and both governments renounce all
claims for war damages originated since August 9, 1945;
(7) talks looking toward a trade and navigation agreement will be begun as soon as possible; (8) the fishing
convention and the agreement for cooperation in rescue
at sea, both signed at Moscow on May 14, 1956, will
enter into force with this declaration; (9) the two countries will cooperate in measures to conserve fish and
other marine resources; (10) the U.S.S.R. agrees to
hand over to Japan the islands of Habomai and Shikotan
after the conclusion of a treaty of peace; (11) negotiations for a peace treaty will be continued after diplomatic relations have been established; (12) this declaration is subject to ratification and will enter into force as
soon as ratifications are exchanged in Tokyo. . . .

Japan's Neutralism

There is something to be said in extenuation of Japan's "neutralism" or, preferably, nonpartisanism. But it need hardly be spelled out, since the fate of Japan as a participant in World War III, should it occur, would be that of Hiroshima many times compounded. The Japanese find it difficult to look beyond such a war to its consequences in the event of a Communist victory. However, they are not in a position, quite apart from their security arrangements with the United States, to be unqualifiedly neutral in the strict sense of neutrality since they agreed at San Francisco "to give the United Nations every assistance in any action it takes in accordance with the Charter and to refrain from giving assistance to any State against which the United Nations may take preventive or enforcement action." This obligation, however, obviously has no reference to nonpartisanism in time of peace nor to a war not involving the United Nations.

In attempting to understand the current policy of Japan one cannot overlook the apparent general desire of her people to be free from the heavy cost of large-scale rearmament and from a revived "Supreme Command" and the militarists' probable renewed interference in every aspect of the political and social order. That this attitude should have arisen in Japan is something of a miracle. In the light of history and of what happened in Germany between the world wars, one might justifiably doubt that it will endure. But the policies of friendly states should be directed toward its encouragement, not toward the revival of militarism. Japan in the role of mediator between democracy and communism—which her statesmen seem to be seeking—may not be

well cast. The conduct of World War II by their prede-
cessors—still fresh in memory—may prompt questions
as to whether they are either sincere in seeking the role
or capable of playing it. Japan's immaturity in her
understanding of liberalism and her penchant for bureaucracy add weight to such questions. She has, however, one qualification that no other people can claim:
she knows from experience what atomic warfare means.

In the contest for the Japanese political mind, democracy is winning over communism; the people have
weighed communism in the balance and found it want-
ing. They have not outlawed it because they are not
afraid of it. Moreover, they came through the postwar
occupation with a sense of gratitude and a feeling of
admiration for Americans, although these sentiments
were mixed with resentment and chagrin. They looked
beneath the surface of the un-Japanese changes that were
imposed upon them and saw that the motivation was
good. Many of these changes will disappear but there
will remain a permanent residue of liberalism. It seems
wise, therefore, to put doubt aside and to afford Japan
an opportunity to attempt the role of nonpartisan and
intermediary. The United States stands to gain thereby.
Democracy is winning not because representatives of
Western peoples have fulsomely proclaimed its superiority to all other ideologies and forms of government
but because the Japanese have found that it is effective
in peace and war and interesting and adaptable at home.
Good works and courteous conduct in personal relations
and recognition of equality in public life are its most
effective advocates. The Japanese are particularly sensi-
tive to criticism and correspondingly responsive to con-
siderate treatment.

Maintaining Japan's Ties with the West

It would seem to be crucially important to capitalize upon the favorable sentiment toward democracy and the West before elements opposed to cooperation with the United States can return to power. Communism and rightist authoritarianism are latent forces of unknown strength. Although in theory at opposite ends of the political spectrum, their distaste for liberalism and internationalism and their liking for violence invite their collaboration against Japan's renovated parliamentary order. That order, while strongly impregnated with bureaucratism, is popular today and has the sincere support of the farmers, organized labor, businessmen and the professional and intellectual classes. The political parties, if not yet cleansed of venality, are vigorous, and elections bring out a larger proportion of voters than is common in many Western states. Emperor Hirohito, more a constitutional ruler and less a mere symbol of authority than the new constitution would suggest, is a reliable bulwark of parliamentarism. . . .

In practical terms this means that any feature of America's present relationship with Japan which affords grounds for charges that our government is treating her as a satellite should be abandoned. It means revision of the security treaty or its termination if that be the desire of Japan. It means non-interference with her foreign policy and greater attention to Japanese views in the administration of the Ryukyus and in the conduct of nuclear weapon tests in the Pacific, to the end that fishermen and the fish upon which they depend for a livelihood and which are an important part of the Japanese diet will not be endangered. It means a trade policy which takes account of Japan's necessity to balance exports against imports. It is incumbent upon Western peoples as well as their governments to recall the disastrous effect of their prewar commercial policies upon Japan, whose economic position today is far less favorable than it was before the war.

If we must assume that Soviet Russia is determined to destroy Western civilization and that she can rely upon the Chinese people to forget their debt to the West and to remember only the indignities suffered by their great country under what Sun Yat-sen termed "hypo-colonialism," the instinct for self-preservation will continue to urge that the present-day world is no place for "neutrals." But it may also be argued that partisanship cannot be compelled and that, should democracy and communism collide, Japan, if treated as an equal by the democracies, will be on their side; also, that her prospects of building up her strength to a significant degree will improve if her economy develops freely through world-wide contacts. It is apparent that Japan is thinking in these terms, while holding firmly to her desire for friendly cooperation with the West, particularly with the United States. Japan, the only country whose constitution prohibits war or armament, and whose geographical situation renders her extremely vulnerable, is quite naturally resolved to contribute her best efforts to the prevention of a third world war in which she would be crushed between the two major opponents.

PRINCIPLES OF JAPAN'S FOREIGN POLICY [2]

Naturally, the direct aim of Japan's foreign policy is to promote our political and economic interests in line

[2] From an address by Foreign Minister Aiichiro Fujiyama to the Foreign Correspondents' Club of Japan, Tokyo, September 5, 1957. Text from *Japan Report*. 3, no 15:2-4. September 10, 1957. Reprinted by permission of the Consulate General of Japan. 3 E. 54th St. New York 22.

with the needs and aspirations of our nation and in the international environment in which our country is placed. But the pursuit of this objective does not in any way mean the sole advancement of our own selfish or exclusive interests. In a world in which interdependence and solidarity among nations have grown to the extent that they have today, it would be unrealistic and to its own disadvantage for a nation to seek to advance its own interests in disregard of those of the other nations of the world. It must be recognized that the pursuit of a self-centered diplomacy has become a thing of the past. . . .

Japan an Asian Nation

Needless to say, a nation's foreign policy is governed by its historical background, geographical position and other factors. Thus we find Japan closely allied, politically and economically, with the United States and the countries of Western Europe. She is perhaps the one nation in Asia that has become most westernized during the past hundred years. Be that as it may, there is no question that Japan is a part of Asia; racially and spiritually the Japanese people are Asian. For instance, an oil painting by a Japanese will have something about it that will distinguish it from that by a French artist. It will retain some quality that is distinctly Japanese from which the Japanese painter cannot break away. And this Japanese quality will, in turn, contain something that is typically Asian in character. It is natural and inevitable, therefore, that Japan's foreign policy should be based on a feeling of kinship and unanimity with Asian countries.

When we speak of Asia, however, we must guard against generalizing, as is often done. We must recognise that the various countries of Asia have different foreign policies arising from their respective historical backgrounds and political and economic positions. But there are certain problems which are common to the Asian countries. One is the rise of nationalism and the resulting resistance against colonialism in whatever form. Another is their aspirations for social and economic progress in order to ensure their newly-won independence. The same can be said for the countries of the Middle East and Africa. As a member of the Asian community, we in Japan strongly sympathize with these aims and aspirations of the peoples of the Asian and Arab countries. We hope sincerely for a peaceful and constructive solution which will make possible the attainment of these aspirations, and we, on our part, wish to contribute in every possible way to such a solution.

Need to Understand Asian Aspirations

Never in her long history has Japan been placed under a foreign colonial rule. Her recent unhappy experience of being placed under foreign military occupation as the result of a war she foolishly waged is, of course, another matter. It may be for this reason that we Japanese sometimes fail to fully understand the discontent and misery of the peoples of Asia who have had to live under colonial rule for a long time. Perhaps we have not made sufficient efforts to try to understand their determination, once having won independence, to build their own future with their own hands, rejecting all outside interference. In the future development of our Asian policy, I am deeply aware that there is need for self-examination, naturally on my own part as Foreign Minister as well as on the part of the Japanese people as a whole. Without doing so, we cannot win their trust and good will as a true friend of Asia.

I believe that the emergence of Asia on the world political scene is an immovable fact and that the smooth conduct of world affairs is impossible if this fact is ignored. In order to make the lofty ideals of world peace and world democracy a reality, Asia's historical significance today must be recognized and Asia's voice must be fully reflected in international affairs. It is from a desire to play a constructive part in this effort that Japan has decided to be a candidate for a seat as a non-permanent member of the Security Council at the forthcoming Twelfth Session of the United Nations General Assembly. [Japan was elected to the Security Council on October 1, 1957.—Eds.]

UNITED STATES SECURITY AND JAPANESE TRADE [3]

For approximately one hundred years, between 1830 and 1930, the United States had generally friendly relations with the nations on the other side of this vast ocean, and we faced no threat from that direction.

Since 1930 there has been a change for the worse. The economic depression of 1929-1930 cut Japan's foreign trade in half. It gave the Japanese extremists a chance to press their program for extending the Japanese Empire. In 1931, Japanese aggression began in Manchuria.

Our Government saw the serious implications of that move. Secretary of State Stimson proposed to other countries that there should be united action to restrain Japanese aggression. The answer, in Secretary Stimson's own words, was "a plain rebuff." Matters went from bad to worse until finally there came Pearl Harbor and

[3] From "Security in the Pacific," speech by John Foster Dulles, Secretary of State, made before the Los Angeles World Affairs Council, June 11, 1954. *United States Department of State Bulletin.* 30:971-3. June 28, 1954.

the Japanese sweep through Southeast Asia and the Western Pacific.

It took four years of terrible war to reverse that situation. Now, happily, the island positions in the Pacific, for the most part, are no longer in hostile hands. Japan is a friendly power. However, on the mainland the situation is different.

When the Japanese surrender occurred, the Russian Red armies were allowed to penetrate deeply into China and Korea to accept the surrender of Japanese forces. Also, the Soviet Government took over the Manchurian railroads and Port Arthur and the Japanese northern islands, as had been agreed at Yalta. But, in violation of its express agreement, the Soviet gave vast Japanese war supplies to the Chinese Communist forces, so that, by the end of 1949, they had gained control of substantially all of the China mainland.

In June 1950 the Communists from North Korea opened their military aggression, and in November 1950 the Chinese Communist regime launched its massive attack against the forces of the United Nations engaged in repelling the Korean aggression. . . .

Today, the vast Pacific is a friendly ocean only because the West Pacific islands and two peninsular positions are in friendly hands. Thus, the United States itself holds Okinawa, Guam, and other islands. Also we have security or defense arrangements covering the Philippines, Australia, New Zealand, Korea, Formosa, and Japan. . . . But close behind this island and peninsular screen lies a mainland with many hundreds of millions of people under a despotic rule that is fanatically hostile to us and demonstrably aggressive and treacherous.

One problem which must particularly concern us is the economy of Japan, a chain of rocky islands whose area is about that of California.

Japan's population, now grown to 87 million, depends for its livelihood upon foreign trade. Trade is offered by the Communists—at a price. The price is that Japan —the only industrial power in Asia—should cease to cooperate with the United Nations and with the United States as it is now doing and should become a work-shop where the abundant raw materials of Asia can be converted into implements for Communist use against the free world. Japan must trade to live, and if the free nations fail to make it possible for Japan to earn its way, then inevitably, though reluctantly, her people would turn elsewhere. This would be stupid from an economic standpoint and folly from a political standpoint. Japan is an excellent customer for our cotton, wheat, and rice. From a political standpoint it requires little imagination to visualize what would happen if Russia, China and Japan became a united hostile group in the Pacific.

It was difficult enough for the United States to defeat Japan when Japan fought alone in the Pacific with China its enemy and Russia neutral. The free world must shun economic policies which would press Japan into becoming the ally or the tool of Communist China and Soviet Russia.

JAPAN: FUTURE ALLY? [4]

Paradoxically, the blustering behavior of Commodore Perry a century ago ushered in a long period of close friendship between the unknown empire of the Tycoon

[4] From "The United States and Japan: A New Century Begins," article by Ralph Braibanti, associate professor of political science, Duke University. *Virginia Quarterly Review*. 31:383-400. Summer 1955. Reprinted by permission.

and the United States. Half a century of tranquility, respect, and friendship was followed, however, by a similar period of suspicion, hurt, and deteriorating diplomacy which reached its nadir with Pearl Harbor. A second century of relations between the United States and Japan now begins and the outset again seems marked by auspicious signs. The visit of former Prime Minister Shigeru Yoshida to the United States late in 1954 was an appropriate symbol of this new era: that he insisted on the visit reveals a feeling of amity; that his visit was opposed by many of his countrymen suggests that the feeling is not universal; that he came as a mendicant diplomat exposes the really precarious and uncertain future which Japan faces.

There can be no certainty that Japan and the United States will remain bound together for the first half or, indeed, for even the first decade of this second century. Japan is one of a group of nations which, less firmly attached to either of the poles of power, can move into new alignments, freshen old enmities, and create new friendships almost as imperceptibly as the drift of desert sands. There are clear and powerful forces which bring our two nations together, yet there are also latent tensions which can push us apart and even rend us asunder. An appraisal of both forces of pull and push seems essential before we can ascertain if cleavage is inevitable or if not, how it can be avoided.

Present Ties

Put in the plainest language, our purpose is to keep Japan from entering the orbit of the Soviet Union's influence. The enthusiasm and even vanity which impelled us a decade ago to attempt to reweave the fabric of Japanese culture into a Jeffersonian cloth of agrarian, rationalist, decentralized design has been almost totally eclipsed by this impelling fact of power politics. The danger of actual conquest by the Soviet Union is not as imminent as the possibility that Japan might be slowly pushed into the vortex of communism by peaceful or even constitutional means. Anxiety over this latter possibility cannot easily be expressed in formal legal arrangements, for no longer do we have any control over the kind of government which Japan evolves. To be sure, there are sinews of international law which bind Japan to the United States, yet economic exigencies or other circumstances can develop new sinews with the Soviet Union and the older connections with our own country can be allowed to wither through disuse.

Present relations between the two nations are constructed on a base of somewhat more than forty legal instruments, five of which can be singled out as being of crucial importance. Three of these five, namely, the Treaty of Peace, the Security Treaty, and the Administrative Agreement, came into force in 1952. The Agreement transferring the islands of Amami-Oshima to Japanese sovereignty was effective in 1953 and the following year the fifth of these important pacts, the Mutual Defense Assistance Agreement, was signed and came into force. Of these, the Peace Treaty is not only the keystone, but, indeed, an important achievement in the progress of international relations. Chief Justice Earl Warren, governor of California during the San Francisco Conference, described it well when he said: "Never before in history have victors been so magnanimous with the vanquished—never before in history have the conquered been so encouraged to regain their normal status of dignity and self-esteem." Prime Minister Yoshida's reference to the treaty as "a magnanimous peace unparalleled in history" is an indication that Warren's judgment was shared by Japan's political leadership. . . .

Anti-Soviet Forces

The currents which seem to propel Japan in a westward direction are from two separate sources. First, there are forces which tend to alienate Japan from the Soviet Union. Secondly, there are positive factors which enhance and deepen understanding and good will with the United States. Among the sources of disaffection between the Soviet Union and Japan, the nature of Japan's experience with the Communist party must be regarded as an important influence. The Communist party was allowed to function without restriction in Japan from 1945 to 1949. It reached the pinnacle of its popularity in 1949 when about ten per cent of the total votes cast were for Communist candidates and thirty-five members of the House of Representatives were Communists. Yet a spectacular repudiation of communism at the polls came in the general election of 1952 when the Communists failed to elect a single member to a seat in the Diet. The underlying causes of this reversal cannot be determined with certainty, but some reasons can be hazarded. Not the least of these was Communist advocacy of abolition of the Imperial Institution at a time when the emperor was enjoying a peak of popularity. This shockingly radical view of the deeply revered Tenno system undoubtedly alienated great numbers of Japanese who might otherwise have found communism appealing. No doubt also the Japanese were appalled by the tactics of riot and bloodshed used by the Communists in 1950. Paradoxical though it may seem, the Japanese have a strongly developed sense of order and peace and regard riot and rebellion as contrary to propriety and therefore as un-Japanese. Further, both the strength and the popularity of the Communists were reduced by MacArthur's justified severity in 1950 when members of the Central Committee were purged and other repressive measures taken. Finally, the invasion of South Korea by Communist forces alerted the Japanese as it did the whole Western world to the deceptions of aggression through indigenous revolt which, since Korea, has become the principal technique of communism.

Such factors reduced the peak membership of some ninety thousand to about seventy-five thousand. . . . In any case the ability of the party to mobilize votes for its own members in national elections has been severely reduced. Yet it would be a mistake to discount the potential influence of the Communist party. . . .

A second determinant in the alienation of the Soviet Union and Japan is the stubborn unwillingness to repatriate Japanese prisoners of war still held in custody by the Communists in Russia, China, and North Korea. This situation has continued for more than ten years with Russians and Japanese disagreeing as to the number of prisoners involved. In September 1954, Japan stated that more than 252,000 Japanese who had never been allowed to return from Communist-held areas had been confirmed as dead. In addition, some 7,000 are thought to be still retained in Communist areas. The net effect of this failure to repatriate has been profound throughout Japan. Almost every village has a family one of whose members has been lost as a result of this policy. To the Japanese the fate of the unrepatriated is one of ignominy, for though separated from the Land of the Gods, they could not share the glory of dying in its defense. This policy of the Communists, deeply affecting the Japanese, has stimulated speculation as to its motivations. The Soviet pattern of action in North

Korea is a frightening example which many Japanese fear may be paralleled. It is now well known that the Soviet occupation of North Korea was managed through the shrewd use of Koreans who had fled to Russia since 1910 and had become naturalized citizens. Such Koreans or their children staffed the new Korean government and became officers and non-commissioned officers in the new North Korean People's Army. A similar cadre of trained Japanese could be very effective in bringing Japan under Communist control. While no proof of this intention can be presented, it is likely that the several thousand Japanese remaining in Communist custody would be more than adequate for any sinister designs which the Communists may have. [Under the terms of the Russo-Japanese joint declaration of October 1956, a small number of Japanese prisoners have been repatriated.—Eds.]

Pro-American Forces

Certain positive forces which tend to push Japan closer to the United States should be assessed. The effect of the seven year occupation has been, generally, to strengthen the ties that bind us together. There will be many who, pointing to widespread anti-American sentiment and dissatisfaction with occupation reforms, may doubt the validity of this appraisal. It is true that immediately after Japan regained her sovereignty there swept across the islands a wave of sentiment against Americans and against everything American. This is hardly a cause for alarm; rather, it was a natural reaction to long control by a nation of dissimilar culture. . . .

The occupation's residue of good will can be accounted for by several factors. In the first place, the Japanese were able to preserve their self-respect when we decided to retain the emperor and to make changes gradually through the existing government. Secondly, the conduct

of Americans was, on the whole, dignified, friendly, and
relatively free of corrupt practices and scandals. Thirdly,
in a significant number of instances the Japanese themselves participated in making many of the policies.
Change could thus be shaped in a Japanese mold and
the base of acceptance broadened. Fourthly, the personal influence and conduct of General MacArthur cannot be discounted. However controversial his personality or other accomplishments may be, he fitted neatly
the Japanese stereotype of leadership. The aristocratic
quality of his command, his intuitive understanding of
the Japanese mind, and the contagion of his classical
dedication to duty were very impressive to the Japanese;
their admiration was inevitably transferred to Americans
and the United States. Fifthly, American action in sav-
ing the Japanese from almost certain starvation in the
early days of the occupation made an indelible impression on the minds of the people and created a burden of
indebtedness. . . . Lastly, the occupation came to a dignified, indeed graceful, conclusion with the peace treaty
admired as a benevolence.

An attitude of identification with the Western powers
was reflected in the platforms of political parties in the
general election of 1952. At that time only one of the
four major parties, the Left-Wing Socialists, took a firm
anti-American attitude. But there was less certainty revealed in the election returns of February 1955, which
returned the interim Hatoyama government. The revi-
sionists (Left and Right-Wing Socialists, Labor-Farmer,
and Communists) who are strongly against rearmament
and favor strengthening ties with Communist China and
the Soviet Union, greatly improved their position by
securing more than a third of the seats in the House of
Representatives. Most of the newly-made voters cast
their ballots for the revisionist parties. For the moment,

at least, Japan has decided to continue her policy of working with the Western powers. But we cannot be as certain what the next moment will bring as we were before the 1955 election.

Potential Threats

The balance which now appears to be somewhat tilted in favor of the West can be upset by several potential sources of tension. Although it is relatively easy to isolate and assess these forces, it is perhaps impossible to predict under what conditions and in what proportions they may interact.

The question of rearmament has been and may continue to be a source of misunderstanding between the two countries. The ninth article of the 1946 constitution, cast as it is in the rhetoric of MacArthur, compels Japan forever to renounce war as a sovereign right. MacArthur felt strongly that this constitutional pacifism would become a feature of Japanese civilization to be copied by the nations of the world. At a moment of defeat and exhaustion, he breathed into the Japanese people the revivifying hope of being the foremost pacifist democracy in the world. None would deny the nobility of this ideal. But the creation of a power vacuum in this strategic area of the Pacific was hardly in accord with the concept of regional security which was then emerging from the United Nations. It has been argued that this proclamation of pacifism was necessary to insure demilitarization of Japan. But Japan's demilitarization was actually accomplished quite independently of any influence of the constitution. Dispersion, if not disintegration, of the military clique (Gumbatsu) and American fiat and continuing surveillance over the manufacture of weapons easily demilitarized the nation. Germany was successfully demilitarized without recourse to constitutional pacifism. When in November 1953 Vice President Nixon characterized Article Nine as a mistake, he made one of the wisest, and certainly the briefest, interpretations ever made of an important constitutional principle. Mistake or not, pacifism succeeded too well. It captivated the imagination of the Japanese, enervated by the privations of war, terrorized by two atomic bombings, and only too eager to renounce war forever. The terrible irony is that the cruel realities of international politics reduced this glorious aspiration to a faded wisp. Yet it has been, at least until now, impossible to excise Article Nine from the constitution. Other constitutional innovations sponsored by the United States conspire against revision. The constitution cannot be amended without popular ratification. Among the voters, for the first time in Japanese history, are women. This newly created portion of the electorate feels most strongly about the ideal of peace. Thus far, Japan's leaders have not dared risk amending the constitution for fear the people might not ratify the proposal. . . .

A second facet of Japanese political thought which must be weighed in assessing the permanence of Japan's identification with the powers of the West is the perennial fascination of the concept loosely called "neutralism." The hope that Japan could remain happily neutral as a Switzerland of the Pacific was especially popular immediately before ratification of the peace treaty in 1952. Neutralism is grounded in part on the conviction that an Asian bloc of nations could effectively serve as a kind of "Third Force" capable of reducing tensions between the West and the Soviet Union. It also results from the uncertainty of continued American loyalty to Japan. The greatest fear is that Japan will be the battlefield of the next war, that Japanese will be simply fodder in the cannons of the great powers. . . .

To a great extent neutralism has lost its captivating force, yet it can find new strength, particularly if fears of nuclear bombing are rekindled. Japan's dilemma of being hopelessly trapped between two world powers is heightened by the unfortunate results of the hydrogen bomb tests on Bikini in March 1954. The death in September 1954, of one of the twenty-three men exposed to radioactive fallout brought a resurgence of Japanese uncertainty and fright. Nor were the Japanese alone in their concern for the effects of radioactivity, for the British House of Commons discussed the subject in November 1954. No doubt our position at the dropping rather than the receiving end accounts for our callous response to the horrors of nuclear bombing. It would do Americans good to read again John Hersey's descriptions in his novel *Hiroshima* and Dr. Takashi Nagai's moving account in *We of Nagasaki*. Many Japanese associate Nagasaki and Hiroshima with other evidences of Caucasian racist notions. Why, they ask, were atomic bombs used in Asia rather than in Europe? The Germans were guilty of scientifically planned bestiality at Dachau, Buchenwald, and elsewhere. The spontaneous atrocities of the Japanese were less in scope and number and different in motivation. In view of the greater guilt of Germany in crimes of inhumanity, it is not difficult for Japanese to regard their selection as atomic bomb victims as but another aspect of a policy of racial discrimination which has included the Gentlemen's Agreement, the Oriental Exclusion Act, the Immigration Act, and the relocation of Japanese citizens from the West coast to government camps. Nor is this feeling dispelled by the cold chronological facts showing that the German surrender occurred in May 1945, before the atom bomb was ready for use. It is difficult for Japanese to believe that American intelligence was so poorly informed that it was not aware that Japan was on the verge of collapse and would have surrendered without resort to atomic bombing.

These deeply felt emotions regarding nuclear bombing have not been adequately assessed in the United States. Our reaction to the radioactive fallout of the spring of 1954, dwelling on the propriety of the Japanese vessels' presence within the danger area, was more quarrelsome than tender. To be sure, we later expressed our sympathies and after the death of the first victim we promptly sent a check for a million yen, and later gave two million dollars as compensation for damages suffered by Japanese. Few episodes in recent times better illustrate the need for articulating diplomatic practices with the emotional, non-rational qualities of Japanese thought. [See "Japan and the H-Bomb," in this section, below.— Eds.]

A third imponderable force which looms ever larger as a real threat to relations between Japan and the United States is the increasingly popular view in Japan that Peiping has found the correct formula for the solution of Asia's problems. . . .

Need for American Understanding

Japan's second century of contact with the West begins with elements of both stability and uncertainty. It is possible that Japan can become the outstanding model of Asian democracy, regaining the confidence of the nations of Southeast Asia, strengthening her defenses, and reweaving strands of Western and Asian culture into her own inimitable fabric of life. Japan could then be the Pacific proof of the capacity of West-

ern constitutionalism to adapt to Asian ways and solve
the problems of Asian nations. Such a possibility is con-
tingent upon Japan's ability to survive, upon the confidence and trust which she can inspire in her Asian
neighbors and upon her trust that the United States
will reciprocate the loyalty which Japan seems to have
pledged to the West. Her survival as an ally of the West
is possible only with American understanding and help;
her standing among her neighbors can come only from
upright behavior made possible by a confident economic
and political security; her trust in the United States will
continue only if we respect her integrity as a nation and
as one of the great civilizations of the world. These
contingencies demand a statecraft of the greatest erudi-
tion and finesse. Nor have these qualities been totally
lacking in our policy toward Japan since the peace treaty.
Should they not be continued and refined, the alternative
would be a Japan lost to the West. Neither right reason
nor self survival can permit the acceptance of this possibility for more than a fleeting moment.

ANTI-AMERICANISM [5]

[In the occupation period] Americans played a big
part in breaking down the deeply ingrained Japanese in-
scrutability. After American armies landed in Japan,
our representatives heartily encouraged Japanese verbal
assaults upon their own most revered customs and leaders, up to and including their emperor. Americans thus
hastened the transformation in Japanese manners which
has produced the current flood of frankness about Americans. This flood was bottled up during the six years

[5] From "The Japs Have Us on the Griddle Now," article by Demaree Bess,
associate editor of the *Saturday Evening Post*. *Saturday Evening Post*. 225:24-5+.
April 4, 1954. Reprinted by permission.

and eight months of our occupation because our military government did not relish criticism of its own activities.

So Japanese publishers accumulated a great storehouse of "revelations" about Americans, and they have handled this material very much as American publishers would do in the same circumstances. In Japan, as in the United States, there are readers for every kind of printed matter, ranging from the cheapest kind of sensationalism to scholarly dissertations. Japan is the only Asiatic country which has taught all its boys and girls to read and write during several generations—as contrasted with 10 per cent literacy in China—and the Japanese have managed to keep all their children in school all through their wars and occupation.

That explains why American behavior in Japan— past, present and future — has been getting such full treatment in recent months from every variety of Japanese publication. The "yellow press," with its particular emphasis upon sex and crime, has been disinterring the private lives of Americans stationed in Japan who were immune from public exposure during the occupation. Apparently some scandal sheets have been hoarding for years stories about romances between high-ranking American occupants and aristocratic Japanese ladies. . . .

Memoirs of "Purged" Leaders

While a considerable part of the recent stream of stories about Americans is thus either deliberately sensational or merely entertaining, most Japanese publishers have aimed at more serious readers. They are finally releasing hundreds of "memoirs"—in books and articles —which were held in reserve during the occupation for fear they might offend the American authorities. Delayed also for many years were the recorded impressions of so-called "purgees"—prominent Japanese leaders who were forbidden to publish anything until recently.

Last summer in Tokyo an American friend suggested to me, only half jokingly, that the so-called purges conducted by Americans probably did more than anything else to improve the quality of Japanese war and postwar memoirs. Washington decided in 1947 to "purge" all Japanese who held top posts between 1931 and 1945 in such activities as politics, finance, industry and journalism. These leaders were forbidden not only to publish anything but also to take any active part in national life. So for several years these immobilized Japanese—some of the brainiest in the country—had plenty of leisure to think about what had happened, was happening and was likely to happen. They became, in fact, a sort of Japanese brain trust, as their memoirs are now revealing, discussing with one another long-range policies for Japan. Some of them also recorded their impressions of developments during and after the war, and they could afford to give much more time to this than Americans who were similarly prominent. The memoirs of our recent leaders, when they have been written at all, usually have been a mere by-product of otherwise crowded days.

These belatedly published impressions by Japanese leaders, including the "purgees," are being read very attentively not only by the Japanese but also by American policy makers. Many purgees are now as active as before the war in politics and industry, in banking and journalism, and their influence is growing, because the Japanese consider that many of them were unjustly treated by Americans. Our policy makers are interested in their present views because, whether we like it or not, the destinies of the United States and Japan are more closely involved than ever before.

I have been reading in translation extensive samples from recently published Japanese memoirs, and one complaint about Americans has reappeared in them time and time again. American behavior seems to be at least as puzzling to Japanese observers as Japanese behavior ever was to us. They describe Americans with such adjectives as baffling, peculiar and unpredictable, and they cite examples which have convinced them that Americans are a curious mixture of hardheaded common sense and quixotic utopianism.

Japanese Impressions of Americans

As an example of our farsightedness, they mention the immense reserve of good will which Americans stored up immediately after the Japanese surrender by treating them with more consideration than they had expected. They express gratitude to General Douglas MacArthur, for protecting them, as they believe, from vengeful Russians, Chinese, Koreans, Australians and Filipinos. Japanese writers present evidence which has convinced them that only American influence prevented widespread starvation in Japan, as other victorious nations demanded withholding of food in 1945, and that Americans also prevented the destruction or removal of industrial plants, without which Japan cannot hope to support its people.

But our occupation was only a few weeks old when Americans began to demonstrate what the Japanese now describe as quixotic utopianism. Our military government, despite the fact that it was headed by conservative-minded General MacArthur, nevertheless launched what seems, in retrospect, a revolution almost as radical as communism. This was no temporary whimsey; for several years a host of American reformers, working under

General MacArthur's command, was given a more or less free hand to abolish the established order in Japan and replace it with an American-type political and social system.

This American project still fascinates Japanese memoir writers far more than anything else which has happened to them in recent times, including their war. All through their accounts runs an incredulous wonder and grudging admiration for the imaginative audacity behind this scheme, even though almost all Japanese now agree that it has failed. They ask themselves why this "American revolution" has fizzled out, and most of them feel that American made the fatal mistake of trying to remold Japan in our own image without taking into account fundamental differences between the two peoples. A veteran Japanese radio executive recalls that Americans put up signs over the washrooms in all buildings which we used, reading, JAPANESE KEEP OUT! He dryly remarks that this sign really summed up our whole reform program, which was a fantastic attempt to create a new Japan out of American heads, whereas no kind of lasting changes in Japan could be made by anybody except the Japanese themselves.

Even more harsh is the judgment of a prominent publisher, Otoku Obama, who writes:

I think the fundamental reason for the failure of reforms introduced by Americans was the absence of any guiding principle in American politics. That explains why such inferior Americans were sent to Japan to handle the affairs of 80 million people. The Japanese would have gained a great deal (especially in industrial reorganization) and would be grateful today to the United States if only more capable American officials had come to Japan. The ignorant and narrow-minded Americans who composed so large a part of the occupation personnel made many mistakes which have been equally harmful to Japan and to the United States. . . .

To a number of Japanese economists and industrialists the most sensational American working for the occupation was a young lady whom they describe as the
"glamorous girl trust buster." The Japanese give this
young woman chief credit for almost halting Japanese
industrial activity. She took a leading part in plans to
dissolve the great Japanese family corporations, known
as Zaibatsu, which have dominated Japan's industry and
commerce for several generations.

Operating on the theory that these family corporations were mainly responsible for Japanese aggression—
a questionable assumption — Washington policy makers
decreed that they should be broken up. The Japanese
were ordered to appoint a liquidation commission, which
was headed successively by Tadao Sasayama and Iwajiro
Noda. In the memoirs of these two men, the American
woman is pictured as the most implacable and persistent
enemy of the Zaibatsu. She spent many months going
through their books.

Mr. Noda comments that the young lady combined
"extremely rigid views" with the charming and vigorous
personality which gave her great influence with top members of General MacArthur's staff. The Japanese are
convinced that this young woman actually wrote the
drastic dissolution decree which they considered ruinous
to their whole economic order. The Japanese were
warned that the American government would not consider a peace treaty until this decree had been accepted.

Mr. Sasayama explains what happened then:

A peace treaty was, of course, the principal objective of
Japanese official policy, and nothing could stand in its way.
So it was up to us to satisfy the American conditions as
smoothly as possible. Fortunately, the Zaibatsu chiefs (who
were supposed to be purged at that time) showed a good

understanding of the problem. We Japanese try to be far-sighted and submissive to the inevitable. This national trait helped to handle the Zaibatsu question without wrecking the country's economy. . . .

American Policy Questioned

An altogether different expression of doubt about American policy in the Far East comes to me in a letter from Tokyo, written by the eminent Japanese historian, Shunkichi Akimoto. . . . As long as I have known Mr. Akimoto he has been a vigorous advocate of a firm working agreement between Japan and the United States, a dangerous position for any Japanese to take between 1931 and 1945. Last summer I asked Mr. Akimoto how he felt now about an American-Japanese working agreement, and he replied that the kind of agreement he once advocated is no longer possible. Neither Americans nor Japanese, he said, seem to have realized the most revolutionary change in the Far East caused by the war—namely, the destruction of Japan as an empire and a military power.

It is therefore foolish, Mr. Akimoto believes, for any Japanese to talk about remaining neutral today. . . . Today the Japanese are almost completely unarmed and cannot even fight to preserve neutrality for many years to come. So the Japanese are offered only two alternatives—to throw in their lot with the United States or to take a minor role in the Soviet system.

When the question is thus reduced to its simplest terms, said Mr. Akimoto, there can be no doubt that the great majority of Japanese prefer a working agreement with the United States—upon one condition. That condition is assurance that Americans now consider themselves a permanent fixture in the Far East, as Russia most certainly is and has been for three centuries. Many Japanese still fear, Mr. Akimoto told me, that Americans will refuse to pay the price of our Far Eastern commitments, and thus leave the field to Russia when we once realize what a long and costly conflict confronts us across the Pacific.

JAPAN AND THE H-BOMB [6]

There is a feeling among the Japanese these days bordering on paranoia that they are the fated victims of American atomic policy. Whenever America lifts an atom, some Japanese gets hurt. Not only did we drop the only two atom bombs ever used against human beings on the Japanese, but they were also the first victims of the H-bomb, in the fall-out at Bikini. To Americans the words *"Fukuryu-Maru"* [the fishing vessel which entered the danger area during the H-bomb test], "Kuboyama" [one of the bomb-dusted fishermen, who died a few months later], and "radioactive tuna" are almost meaningless collocations of sounds; but to the Japanese they have become household words that stir a deep sense of resentment. It is true, of course, that American soldiers and Marshall Islanders were also affected by the fall-out. But most Japanese do not know about this—nor do they want to know. If asked, they would argue that it is your business if you hurt "your own" people; but you have no right to jeopardize others. Besides, most Japanese prefer to think of themselves as unique, the privileged victims, and they do not want to share the spotlight with American GI's or Marshallese natives. As Professor Ikutaro Shimizu of the Gakushuin University said in an argument that seems to be very persuasive to Japanese

[6] From an article by Herbert Passin, research associate with the Department of Sociology and Anthropology, Ohio State University. *Bulletin of the Atomic Scientists.* 11:289-92. October 1955. Reprinted by permission.

intellectuals, twenty-three fishermen may seem like a
small number compared to the hundreds of thousands
of Hiroshima and Nagasaki victims, but in a symbolic
sense it is even worse. "During the war, Japan and
America were enemies. But this time, the injury was
done to an ally, or at least to a friendly nation." . . .
This is, to be sure, somewhat disingenuous of Professor
Shimizu because he has been devoting a good part of his
intellectual activity to persuading people *not* to be
friendly to America; but whatever the source of the
argument, it holds great appeal for the Japanese.

What we sense immediately here in Japan is that
Americans and Japanese are looking at this problem in
a different way, that they are not on the same wave
length. For Americans, the problems created by the
Bikini fallout were essentially technical. The explosion
was enormous; the fall-out exceeded calculations. Since
the consequences were quite unintentional, it is enough
to estimate the amount of the damage and make proper
compensation. For the Japanese, however, the problems
were emotional. Why are we always the victims? Are
we destined to suffer from every contact we have with
America? Does this not show America's contempt for
us? In addition, there was something peculiarly horrify-
ing in the prospect that fish, Japan's main protein source,
might be contaminated by radioactivity.

The Fukuryu-Maru Wall

There was, therefore, a complete lack of congruence
in American and Japanese reactions, both sides failing to
understand or to recognize the sincerity of the other.
Whatever the Americans said inevitably sounded like an
insult to the Japanese, since it was technical and rational
and seemed to regard feelings and anxieties as irrelevant,

Many things that we did, however well meaning they may have seemed at home, were wrong in the emotional atmosphere of Japan at the time. When Japanese doctors requested certain information on radioactivity, for example, the Americans refused it on the grounds that it was "unnecessary" for the treatment of radioactive burns. As Professor Shigeo Oketani of Tokyo Engineering University said, the Americans may very well have been right, but "probably nothing has made Japanese people who were originally friendly to America incline a favorable ear to the fashionable anti-Americanism of intellectual circles more than this refusal." . . .

The American statement, however correct it may have been, was not on the same emotional wave length as the Japanese request. Professor Tetsuzo Tanikawa, Dean of the Faculty of Literature of Hosei University, a leading proponent of world government, speaks for much Japanese sentiment when he says:

I am not what is called an "anti-Americanist." . . . I . . . have long been censuring Russia's attitude toward world government. But today I must censure America as well. . . . We are informed that American newspapers dealt with the Bikini incident only as a problem of leakage of secrets. And Chairman Cole of the Joint Congressional Committee on Atomic Energy reportedly said that it was possible that the Japanese fishermen had been spying on the test. This plain national egoism has completely forgotten respect for the lives of the unfortunate fishermen and the danger threatening the daily life of the Japanese people. We cannot but conclude that this comes from a subconscious contempt for colored people. . . .

This disparity in emotional tone can be seen at every step. The first American reaction was that perhaps the *Fukuryu-Maru* had run too close to the danger area. Perhaps it was spying. If not, what was it doing so close to the blast? For responsible officials who must take into consideration all possibilities, this is undoubtedly a perfectly reasonable speculation. But speculating in public, as high-placed Americans do all too often, can have disastrous effects that cannot be effaced by official statements. The possibility of spying, for example, was probably not seriously entertained. And as it turned out, it was very quickly rejected. But its very announcement was enough to cause harm, and its retraction was unable to overcome the resentment it had caused. For some reason the charge was especially galling to Japanese sensitivities, and it opened the way to a flood of resounding denunciations in the press of American "arrogance" and laborious proofs that the charges were false. Learned articles appeared both in the academic and the popular press to demonstrate that even on the evidence as given —and it was strongly hinted that much was kept back by the Americans for security reasons—the fishermen must have been outside the danger area.

. . . [On] April 18, 1954, Ryuzaburo Taguchi, President of the Color Film Research Institute, argued, for example, that sound waves of explosive origin travel faster than ordinary sound waves, and that given the temperature of the Marshall Islands and the size of the explosion, the sound would have reached the distance claimed by the fishermen in 6 minutes 15 seconds. Then when the American side accepted—with what seemed to the Japanese considerable reluctance—the conclusion that the ship was actually beyond the designated area, the American reaction was again a "correct" and rational one: this confirms that the fall-out was greater than expectations; the problem must be studied. It was this feeling that the Americans were concerned only with the technical aspects of the problem and that they disregarded the damage to Japan that outraged Japanese sentiment.

In Japanese eyes, the American reaction appeared surly and ungracious. "Why didn't the fishermen report what happened right away?" we asked. If they had washed the ashes off immediately, the results would not have been so serious. All perfectly reasonable observations. But we were being querulous and logical when the situation called for demonstrating one's sympathy; technical issues should have taken second place in these first reactions.

The Tuna Economy

The problem of the "radioactive tuna" shows the same lack of communication. The Americans seemed to take the attitude that the Japanese were being unnecessarily hysterical. Again, although the American may have been right, the statement could only sound cold and unfeeling. For one thing, Americans are unable to comprehend how important fish is to Japan and therefore how terrifying to basic security this anxiety about contamination can be. It is true that anti-American elements deliberately inflated the issue, but they were able to do so because it did touch on primordial sensitivities of the Japanese people. For Americans, Pacific tuna is a canned delicacy that is nice to have but that we can do without. For Japanese, fish from the Pacific is a daily necessity.

But there is another aspect of the problem that Americans do not understand. Since the end of the war, Japanese fishermen have been having a hard time. Their traditional fishing areas have been cut off on all sides: the Russians have taken their best fishing grounds in the north, right down to within two miles of the coast of the home island of Hokkaido; the Chinese have cut off important fishing waters on the west; the South Koreans have established the "Rhee Line," and all Japanese vessels caught beyond it are impounded and their crews interned; and many of the Central Pacific fisheries in the former mandated islands are now under American control. So anything that appears to threaten their livelihood is a very serious matter, and since there are more than a million fishermen in Japan, this anxiety spreads itself to all corners of the country.

A young fisherman in Chiba Prefecture expressed what is undoubtedly a widespread view:

I was repatriated from the Soviet Union in the autumn of 1948. So far, I have been very grateful for America's policy toward Japan. But since this H-bomb business I find that in spite of myself I am more sympathetic to the Communist position. . . . It is outrageous for the Chairman of the Congressional Atomic Energy Committee to suggest that the *Fukuryu-Maru* fishermen were spies. The American Army here in Japan has taken over the Kujukurihama Coast for a firing and maneuver ground; and then when fishermen move out to the deep seas to try to make their living, important fishery grounds there are turned into H-bomb proving areas.

For several years now the American Army has been engaged in a dispute with local fishermen on a stretch of beach known as Kujukurihama over artillery practice in the area. The fishermen claim that the firing harms their catch, while the Americans contend that they need the area for training purposes. Both sides are probably right.

What made the American attitude seem particularly insincere was that no sooner had the Americans made the suggestion that the Japanese were perhaps being overanxious about the radioactivity of the tuna when the American tuna packers announced that they would not accept Japanese tuna for the time being—because it might be contaminated!

Medical Misunderstandings

When the injuries to the fishermen became known, Ambassador Allison offered his condolences on behalf of the United States government. But by the time these official condolences were transmitted, it was almost too late. The impression of American "coldness" was already firmly fixed by the initial reactions of Americans reported in the press.

Then came one of the worst mistakes of all. As a friendly gesture, the Americans offered the use of the facilities of the Atomic Bomb Casualty Commission (ABCC) in Hiroshima. Now this offer could only be based on a complete misreading of Japanese sentiment. The ABCC had been established in Hiroshima and Nagasaki by the United States Atomic Energy Commission as a research institution. From its very foundation, the Japanese have resented the fact that it was designed for diagnosis and research but not for treatment. The American government has campaigned for years to convince the Japanese that the ABCC was not set up for treatment and that this was as it should be. The findings of objective scientific investigation, we argued, would in the long run benefit the Japanese people as much or more than mere treatment. But the Japanese have never fully given up their suspicions that they are being used as "guinea pigs" by the ABCC. Therefore to offer the ABCC facilities after all this suggested one of two things: that the original contention that the ABBC could not provide treatment was untrue; or that the Americans wanted these fresh cases for research purposes. Neither conclusion was to our benefit. Said the [newspaper] *Shukan Asahi* on April 4, 1954, "The ABCC has never once treated A-bomb sufferers in Hiroshima and Nagasaki with kindness, and it treats the patients as 'guinea pigs.' " When Dr. Morton of the ABCC visited Tokyo University Hospital, it was taken for granted by Japanese that he had not come on a visit of sympathy or cooperation, but simply to do some research on the secondary symptoms of H-bomb radioactivity. Dozens of articles in the press appeared on the general theme that "We are not guinea pigs!"

Thus every action meant something different to the two sides. The Americans, for example, offered to make a joint medical investigation. From an American point of view this may have looked like cooperation, but from a Japanese point of view it smacked of insult to the Japanese medical profession. They immediately interpreted the offer to mean that the Americans were going to challenge the Japanese diagnoses and estimates of damage, perhaps in order to reduce the extent of America's financial liability. The Japanese were indignant. "We know more about radioactive burns than anyone else in the world, including the Americans. We are the only people in the world who have been exposed to atomic radiation on a large scale." Therefore, Japanese medical circles, interpreting our offer of cooperation and of ABCC facilities to imply distrust of their ability, were bitterly offended. Dr. Kazuo Miyoshi of the Okinaka Internal Department, Toyko University Hospital, in a medical report on the condition of the twenty-three fishermen, said coldly:

We are glad to have American good will. But this can only be on a collaboration basis, not a joint-study basis. We have never refused to allow American doctors to examine the patients. But we did not want them interrogating patients for three or four hours at a time because the patients need a good rest and they are worried about being used as guinea pigs. , , ,

Unfortunately, this sensitivity has been rubbed raw by a continuing series of statements made by American doctors, private and governmental, expressing doubts about the Japanese diagnosis of the causes of the death of Aiichiro Kuboyama, one of the bomb-dusted fishermen, on September 23, 1954. The suggestion has been made that the cause of death may not have been radioactivity, but rather jaundice resulting from a transfusion infection. Whether this is true or not—and American statements are only suggestions of alternative possibilities—they rub everybody the wrong way because of their clear implication that Japanese doctors are incompetent. In the latest of this series, Dr. Berry repeats the charges. . . . Since Dr. Berry is in the Defense Department, the Japanese regard his statement as the official statement of the United States government, and no amount of denial will convince them otherwise. Japanese medical circles have therefore turned with warm relief to the more sympathetic statement of three foreign doctors on June 1, 1955, at the International Radiation Conference in Hiroshima—which had an anti-American flavor and was not attended by Americans. Dr. Simon Sevitt, pathologist from Birmingham, England, Dr. Leonardo Guzman, Director of the National Institute of Radium of Chile, and Dr. Karl Holubec, Czech surgeon, agreed that the Japanese diagnosis was correct and that there were no grounds for the American doubts. . . .

United States and Soviet Tests

The net result has been a strong feeling against American atomic and thermonuclear experiments. It is true that the Russians conduct them too, and it is even true that Japan was bothered by "radioactive rains" on its Japan Sea side as a result of the Russian explosions of middle September and late October 1954. But in spite of the attempts of cooler heads to put these matters in perspective, there is without doubt a tendency to consider the United States more at fault than Russia. The Russians conduct their tests on their own territory. But the American tests are held in the Pacific. By what right does America use the Pacific Ocean for its own experiments which endanger Japan and her food sources? America is violating the freedom of the sea by denying its use to other nations.

"The Pacific is not an American lake!" announced the *Shukan Asahi* in its April 4, 1954, issue, echoing the *Daily Herald* of London. Learned jurists, lawyers, and professors filled the press with detailed analyses of the position of the tests in international law. Fuel was added to the flames by the statement of the Secretary of the House Atomic Energy Committee, Nichols, that experiments would continue in spite of Japanese protests. Koichi Fukui, a member of the radioactivity team that went to Bikini in May 1954, expressed the views of many Japanese when he said:

It is impermissible to contaminate the sea by H-bomb tests when no one has any idea of what its effects will be. The American scientists did not really know, whatever they may claim. . . . Two months after the explosion, the fish were still dangerously radioactive. . . .

America and the Atom

America's failure to meet the emotion of Japanese reaction has led to the charge that we are cruel and inhuman, perhaps, in the suspicion given voice by Professor Tanikawa, because we are fundamentally contemptuous of "colored people." It must be remembered that throughout Asia, and particularly in India, it is widely believed that America dropped the first atom bomb on Japan, rather than on Germany, because the

Japanese are "colored people" and the Germans are "whites." No amount of argument will convince people that the atom bomb was only developed after the German surrender. And if America is capable of such inhumanity, "treating the masses like animals," in the words of the novelist Kojoro Serizawa . . . then perhaps the Communist charges of germ warfare in Korea are also true. . . .

With this background, it is understandable that the Japanese become jittery whenever the words "American" and "atomic" appear in the same sentence. So when Americans come, atom in hand, to make an offer, there is a strong inclination to look long and hard. It was this mood that lay behind the protracted hassle over our offer of enriched uranium to Japan, which was part of President Eisenhower's "atoms-for-peace" program. Once again America found itself in the ridiculous position of offering gifts to people who were not at all certain that they wanted to receive them. Although the offer was welcomed by engineers and businessmen, most scientists were very suspicious and inclined to reject it. The debate raged in scientific and academic bodies—providing the staple of Japan Science Council deliberations for weeks on end—in the press, and in the Diet committees, and bitter sentiments were expressed on all sides. The issue divided the country politically, with the Right and the Left Socialists (not to mention the Communists and the Farmer-Labor party) opposed, and the conservative parties more or less in favor.

Although many specific points of objection were raised, what the debate showed was something more important: a real distrust of American atomic policy. Speaking of the American offer, which he characterized as the "American atomic energy offensive," Professor Koji Fushimi, physicist of Osaka University, argued that the United States is motivated by the desire to divert world opposition to the military uses of atomic energy by emphasizing its peaceful uses; to support its domestic armament industry; to assure overseas supplies of uranium; and to capture markets for her atomic energy industry. . . . The consequence of cooperation with the United States in electric power generation by atomic energy [one of the proposals involved in the uranium offer] would be the domination of all of Japanese industry by American monopoly capitalism through the manipulation of electric power prices. . . .

Although an agreement was finally signed between the Japanese and American governments on June 21, 1955, the opposition of the "progressive front"—of scientists, intellectuals, socialists, and trade unionists—has succeeded in leaving the impression that this was not a generous American gift, but just something else America has forced down Japan's throat.

This attitude is, of course, strengthened by the growing political hostility toward American foreign policy here and the recent moves to "normalize" relations with Russia and China. . . .

Revising Our Policies

In respect to atomic policy, what this means is that many people are becoming more favorable to the Communist bloc. A favorable attitude toward Communist atomic policy seems to be psychologically the necessary counterpart of the resumption of "normal" relations. This feeling coincides with the growing Russian and Chinese campaign to woo Japanese intellectuals, a campaign that has been having striking success. . . .

It is this mood that American atomic policy must take into account in future dealings with Japan. We cannot act in international relations on the basis of purely rational and technical calculations of what we think is good for people. . . . From a narrow point of view, the problem is essentially one of public relations. This is supposed to be our specialty, but we still cannot present the face to the world that we want to present. But from a larger point of view, the problem is how to make manifest the feelings of a whole people, their spontaneous warmth and sympathy. That is why the warm personal gestures—the treatment of the "Hiroshima maidens," or the meeting together of people in international conferences—have more effect at certain moments in history than the giant official actions. As long as America held undisputed lead in atomic development, we could get away with unilateral actions. But resentment against our policy now has other places to turn. The Japanese reaction should alert us to the dangers before it is too late.

THE BONIN ISLANDS: PAWNS IN A POWER GAME [7]

An ominous question mark hangs over the future of the 178 persons comprising the civilian population of the tiny Bonin Islands.

The inhabitants want to become United States citizens, but have become, instead, pawns in an international game.

The Bonins are sheer, grim volcanic outcroppings in the western Pacific, about midway between Japan and the United States island territory of Guam. Hundreds of miles from regular shipping lanes, they have been islands of mystery except to officials and others who have lived

[7] From "Bonin Isles' 178 Civil Residents Seen as Pawns in Power Game," by Robert Trumbull, chief of the New York *Times* Tokyo bureau. New York *Times*. p 1+. March 11, 1956. Reprinted by permission.

in the lonely jungle clearings. Occasional visitors in whaling and fishing craft were almost exclusively Japanese nationals until the end of the World War II. . . . .

The islands figure prominently in the postwar contentions that inevitably followed Japan's resumption of technical sovereignty over them with the United States continuing in military occupation.

The question, as far as the islanders are concerned, is whether they shall remain under the jurisdiction of the United States, now represented by a dilapidated and undermanned naval station on the main island of Chichi, or whether they shall revert to the unwelcome rule of the Japanese.

Conflicting Claims

The Japanese claimed the islands eighty years ago, ignoring the assertions of the settlers that they were Americans.

Most of the tightly inbred island fishing and farming community today claims relationship, either by direct descent or through intermarriage, to Nathaniel Savory, a Massachusetts seafarer who settled here in 1830, when the Bonins were uninhabited and unclaimed. He died in 1874. . . .

International considerations that may affect the eventual fate of this strange community in the far Pacific are these:

Japan wants the United States to permit 7,711 former Japanese residents of the islands to return, partly because this matter has become a national issue in Japan, and partly because this would give Japan a lever on the Soviet Union for return of the Kuriles and other former Japanese territories held by the Russians.

The United States Navy, administering the islands for Washington under a security agreement with Japan, apparently has long-range plans for an important submarine base in the Bonins, and wants no Japanese settlers complicating the situation. The present residents heartily concur in discouragement of the Japanese, albeit for different reasons that are economic and political.

Eager to strengthen United States ties with Japan, but also mindful of prospective relations between Tokyo and Moscow, the United States State Department appears to be supporting the case of the Navy and the "indigenous" islanders without real conviction.

Spokesmen for the former islanders now residing in Japan evince impatience with the Navy's contention that resettlement of the Bonins would compromise military security. They declare that a Japanese population in the Bonins would be no more of a security risk than those near United States bases in Japan and Okinawa.

The Navy, in rebuttal, cites the smallness of the islands and the necessity of supplying any civilian settlers through the only port, which is on Chichi and is the heart of the military base.

All the adult islanders, simple fishermen and farmers with names like Gilley, Robinson, Webb and Washington, unanimously signed a petition to the State Department a year ago. It opposed Japanese resettlement on the grounds that the 7,711 listed as wishing to return "are mostly immigrants of the early 1930's and are not true Bonin Islanders."

The petition added that "only a nominal percentage of these would be able to subsist on the natural resources of the islands and the surrounding waters." The rest, the petition said, worked for the Japanese military.

Later, the islanders sent a delegation of four persons to Washington to plead their case. Meanwhile, the islanders as a group have twice requested United States citizenship, without result.

Historical Background

The Bonin Islanders legally are Japanese nationals. In the peace treaty signed in San Francisco in 1951, the United States recognized Japan's "residual sovereignty" over the Bonins and Okinawa. These islands were left under United States military government for an indefinite time in a concurrent agreement on Pacific security.

Japan's historical claim to the Bonins goes back to a visit there by Sadayori Ogasawara in 1593, just fifty years after the Spanish navigator Don Ruy Lopez de Villalobos was said to have sighted the islands for the first time on record. The Japanese named the group Ogasawara Gunto, but did not get around to asserting sovereignty until 1876.

Tokyo's annexation of the tiny group was not disputed by anyone at that time except Nathaniel Savory and his little band who had been on Chichi (then called Peel Island) for forty-six years. In 1853 Commodore Matthew Perry, who called at Chichi on his historic voyage to open up Japan, strongly recommended that the United States acquire the Bonins, but he was disregarded.

Until the time of World War II, the Caucasian blood of the original colonists had been mixed with that of Malayan, Japanese, Polynesian and Negro stock. Chichi had become a principal Japanese submarine base and one of the strongest fortifications in the Pacific.

The Bonins, originally so called through a corruption of the Japanese name Bune Shima, or Islands Without

Men, now teemed with 25,000 or more soldiers, more than 7,000 Japanese civilians and the little community that still defiantly regarded itself as American. . . .

In 1944, under intensive American bombing, all but the military personnel were evacuated to Japan. After the war, United States occupation authorities repatriated the Savory clan and the other descendants of pre-Japanese colonists. The others were barred.

The Japanese, the Islanders, and the United States Navy

The League of Bonin Evacuees for Hastening Repatriation also sent a delegation to Washington last year with powerful Japanese political backing. It asserted that before World War II these now nearly destitute refugees had earned in the islands nearly $2 million a year by farming, nearly $1 million by fishing, and nearly $500,000 by whaling.

While these Japanese figures could not be checked, most of the many Bonin Islanders interviewed . . . [on Chichi] agreed that the hard-working Japanese settlers had prospered in the islands. Now it is they who are prospering by sending produce to Guam through a cooperative trading company. But that is not the only reason they do not want the Japanese back.

"The Japanese, while treating us fairly until the war, always regarded us with contempt because we weren't Japanese," said Charles Washington, stately descendant of a Negro who left an American whaling ship here in the early 1840's. The islanders fear worse discrimination because of their present pro-American stand.

The Tokyo Government wishes to set up a complete civil administration in the Bonins. The United States

Navy, like the islanders, views the prospective complications with disquiet.

The two top Navy officers here are . . . veteran submariners who view the Bonins as a potentially important base for undersea craft. . . .

Many United States submarines have made Chichi a port of call since the war. In time of hostilities in the Pacific they could replenish their torpedoes and other supplies here, as the Japanese once did.

OKINAWA: UNITED STATES WARD IN THE PACIFIC [8]

Sakini, the wily Okinawan interpreter in *The Teahouse of the August Moon,* observes in the preamble to the play that the process of learning from the conqueror is "sometimes painful." And sometimes, as is happening on Okinawa today, it is the conqueror who suffers the pain. It came as a sharp jolt to the Americans who have tutored Okinawans in democracy for nearly twelve years when the voters of Naha, the capital, recently elected as their mayor Kamejiro Senaga, a reputed Communist who had campaigned largely on a platform of "Yankees, Go Home!"

Some Americans here believe that if affairs were handled right in Washington, this tiny island [of the Ryukyu chain] with its wholly Oriental indigenous population, would be "a showcase for American democracy in the East." It is so far from that today, however, that the authorities considered it wise to cancel plans for an international conference of Asian educators this year at the American-instituted University of the Ryukyus in

[8] From "Okinawa: 'Sometimes Painful' Lesson for Us," article by Robert Trumbull, chief of the New York *Times* bureau in Tokyo. New York *Times Magazine.* p29+. April 7, 1957. Reprinted by permission.

Naha. They feared that the visitors, especially those from neutralist countries, might be so influenced by critical elements that they would go home as propagandists for the return of the Ryukyus to Japan.

There is little outward evidence of unfriendliness to Americans in Okinawa. When you drive through a village laughing children hail you with beaming smiles and screams of "Hello, baby!" which they apparently have come to think is the standard American greeting. Like their Japanese cousins, Okinawans are invariably polite, but they have an independence of character which often leads them to go their way in defiance of the conqueror. A visitor to the villages will find that these people think and discuss critically the problems of the day with greater sophistication than the average American is likely to suspect.

Citizenship Status

A paramount problem for most Okinawans appears to be their anomalous political status as citizens of Japan and wards of the United States. One high-ranking American here describes the Okinawans as "people without a flag" and suggests that much apparent anti-Americanism on the island may be largely the product of their feeling of insecurity.

The Ryukyuans, who speak a dialect Japanese and have been attuned to Japanese culture since their incorporation into that empire as a prefecture in 1876, say frankly that they feel like Japanese and want to revert to Tokyo's rule. They still nurture many grievances against the repressive regime they knew until the American forces captured the island in April 1945 in one of the bloodiest battles of the Pacific. But they also believe that relations with the Japanese, themselves newly democratized under American influence, would be different today.

Economic Problems

Another yearning that disturbs the Okinawans is the yearning for land. Their island, sixty-seven miles long and from three to twenty miles wide, has a population density about twenty-two times that of the United States, or about 1,270 persons a square mile to 54. A congressional land committee which visited here last fall estimated in its report that if the United States were as crowded as Okinawa, her population would be 2.75 billion—more people than there are on earth.

Since the island contains only 80,000 acres of tillable land—one acre for every seven and a half persons—the Okinawans were understandably exercised when the United States armed forces took about one cultivable acre of every five for military use. The construction of an eighteen-hole golf course for personnel also started a controversy between the Army and Okinawan farm organizations. The farmers say they can understand appropriating farm land for military purposes, although they may not like it. But they do not understand taking their crop land for amusement. The Army's answer is that the former occupants of the golfing area are now making more by working on the links than they ever earned from their farms.

In the long dispute over appropriation of farmland the United States, it appears now, has met every objection but one. Rent to be paid by the United States was tripled; lump-sum compensation for long-term use at least doubled. A development fund in which Okinawan owners may invest their money and earn a perpetual income may be set up, resettlement programs are afoot and, finally, the United States is leaving actual title to the land with the Okinawan owners, who, in theory, may hope some day to return to it.

But the problem turned out to be more than economic. Okinawans, the Americans discovered, have a fanatical attachment to their land that is akin to religion. Land has been the core of their social organization as well as their livelihood and, before the Americans came, transfer of land from one owner to another was rare. No way has been found to compensate for this love of the land.

A third grievance of the Okinawans stems from their work on Army projects. The United States construction program and the expenditure of more than $4 million a month by the armed forces sustain the island economy. The armed forces currently employ more than 50,000 Okinawans—more than half the total labor force. About 10,000 Okinawan girls find work as domestics in American quarters and many other islanders find jobs in local industries that have sprung up with the military expansion.

But the pay of Okinawans in defense work, set by a military wage board in faraway Washington, is very low; it ranges from 10 cents an hour minimum for a heavy laborer to 36 cents maximum for a skilled foreman. The Okinawan is embittered, not only because an American doing the same work receives up to twenty times as much, but also because an imported Japanese employee may be getting five to ten times the pay of his Okinawan counterpart, although retail prices of a range of daily needs are said to average 28 per cent more here than in Japan.

Okinawa today is a combined "Little America" and "Little Japan." Most of the 40,000 Americans, service men and dependents on the island live in a different world from the 600,000 "indigenous personnel," as service gobbledygook calls the islanders.

Defense Installations

From a height on the island one can see the twin white ribbons of Kadena Air Base's two 12,000-foot concrete runways, longest in the Far East and capable of accommodating any plane in the Air Force inventory. The other major air installation is outside Naha, where civilian transocean airliners landing and taking off during daylight hours are required to have their window curtains drawn, according to United States security regulations.

These and several subsidiary airfields, the naval headquarters of the Taiwan (Formosa) Straits Command, the Third Marine Division's barracks, vast forests of antennas for far-ranging communications installations and a network of radar-guided anti-aircraft gun emplacements on a round-the-clock alert—these are the visible heart of the $588,600,000 United States defense bastion on Okinawa. There are also immense storage areas and underground secret chambers believed to contain atomic bombs. In this panorama of military might lies the reason the United States retained Okinawa and the other Ryukyu Islands, a prefecture of Japan, when the occupation ended in 1952. These defenses are why we show every indication of meaning to stay for as long as anyone can foresee.

The military installations are enclosed by miles of high steel-mesh fencing, guarded in some places by fierce dogs trained to attack any unknown intruder. Barring occasional destructive typhoons and a certain amount of island claustrophobia, life for Americans behind these fences is considered good by Army standards. Officers, higher-grade enlisted men and civilian employees of the United States Government who have families here are generally quartered in attractive concrete houses, more or less typhoon-proof. Their nightly television is broadcast by an Air Force station from filmed stateside network programs, commercials included. They can also tune in the Armed Forces radio and Okinawan stations. . . .

Many service families, paying one or more maids around $20 a month to do the cooking and other housework, look back on high-priced though possibly substandard housing, a complete lack of domestic help and other undesirable features of many stateside assignments and consider Okinawa a "good deal"; so much so, in fact, that the Army has felt it necessary to limit Okinawa tours to three years.

Okinawan Life

From one of these self-contained American communities it is not very far in miles over a good highway—mostly paved and some portions four-lane—to a village like Nakagusuku, under the hill where the castle of Okinawan kings once stood. But it's a long way—and all downhill—in other respects.

Here, in conditions approximating those of the average Okinawan, you find a crowded cluster of thatched, one-room shacks lacking running water and elementary sanitation. Chickens wander among the littered huts, a pig squeals from an enclosure of rushes. Some of the older women, mashing sweet potatoes to yellow pulp with mallets in old wooden bowls, have floral and other designs tatooed on their fingers. You chat with a man, the head of a family, and find that his whole day's wages wouldn't have paid for your $1.50 dinner in the club last night.

But the experienced Asian traveler notes that the apparent standard of living here, while lower than the average in Japan, is far better than in most rural villages in India and a dozen other countries of the Far East. The villagers are eating rice every day, which they could seldom afford a few years ago. They have shoes and clothes that hundreds of millions of other Asians would envy. And here are a schoolhouse and community hall of permanent construction and a playground—facilities that most Indian villages are only now getting, one by one, under the Community Development Plan.

The Okinawan knows that he is better off than he was before the Americans came and he is also aware— as he will readily tell you—that conditions on Amami Oshima, in the northern Ryukyu group returned to Japan in 1953, have become a great deal worse since the Americans left. Yet because he is confronted daily with examples of the highest standard of living in the world he thinks he should be doing even better than he is.

Among Okinawa's three political parties, there is little difference in principle on domestic issues—all are for reversion of Okinawa to Japan sooner or later and all oppose the American land policy. The Communists and their supporters, however, differ from the others in demanding that the Americans get out right now. Few Okinawans appear to be serious about this. The Democrats, who are the dominant and conservative party, and the Socialist Masses party, which is the principal opposition, favor letting Americans stay on after reversion by arrangement with the Japanese Government, on the same basis as they now remain in Japan itself. . . .

American Policy

Many Americans here believe that the United States should give long and careful thought to ways of countering the Communist-led exploitation of Okinawan grievances and frustrations. It is widely said by Okinawans as well as Americans that continual agitation for reversion to Japan would abate if Washington were to say that abandonment of the Ryukyus would not be considered for a stated number of years. Many also think that Washington should initiate a thoughtfully conceived, long-range program for economic and social development to replace the more or less limited and uncertain operation that has been in effect since 1945.

Jugo Thoma, the Army-appointed chief executive of the locally manned government of the Ryukyu Islands, believes that as time goes on and if conditions continue to improve, the anxiety of Okinawa for reversion to Japan will lessen. At any rate, Mr. Thoma, a former judge and Naha city mayor, urges Okinawans to reconcile themselves to the expectation that the United States will hold onto Okinawa for another generation at least.

In the long run, the policy of the United States administration of the island appears to foreshadow a drastic reconstruction of an ancient way of life. Lieutenant General James E. Moore, United States Army deputy governor and supreme authority on the island, has urged dramatic development of industries to replace an agricultural economy that has always been a poor one and can only become more inadequate with the population growing by 20,000 a year.

Thoughtful Okinawans are urging the United States to sponsor an intensive emigration program to other countries and perhaps to the many islands of the Pacific Trust Territory administered by the United States as sole United Nations trustee. Many, in agreement with some Americans, believe Washingon should embark on a "crash" program of social betterment along Point Four principles to make Okinawa really a "showcase." And a majority, it appears, believe we fail to practice what we preach when we refuse to let Okinawans elect their chief executive. As Sakini said, "Okinawans most eager to be educated."

THE FACTS OF THE GIRARD CASE [9]

The United States agreed . . . that a Japanese court should try an American soldier charged with having killed a Japanese woman.

The soldier is Army Specialist 3/c William S. Girard, twenty-one years old, of Ottawa, Illinois.

. . . [On January 30, 1957] Girard fired an empty cartridge case from a grenade launcher to frighten away several Japanese scavenging for metal on the firing range at Somagahara. Mme. Naka Sakai, forty-six years old, was hit in the back by the shell case and killed.

In a joint statement issued at the Pentagon . . . Secretary of Defense Charles E. Wilson and Secretary of State John Foster Dulles said that Girard's action "was not authorized" and therefore was not done in the performance of duty.

Consequently, the two officials said that they had concluded that the trial of Girard in Japanese courts was "in full accord" with an agreement between Japan and the United States governing the status of American forces in Japan.

[9] From "U.S. Agrees to Let Japanese Try G.I. in Woman's Death," by E. W. Kenworthy, of the New York *Times* Tokyo Bureau. New York *Times.* p 1+. June 5, 1957. Reprinted by permission.

The question of jurisdiction in the Girard case has become a heated issue in the Japanese press and has inflamed public opinion.

The Government's decision in the Girard case came less than two weeks after the destructive anti-American rioting in Taipei, Taiwan. The rioters, who sacked the United States Embassy and the United States Information Agency building, were angered by a United States Army court-martial's acquittal of a sergeant accused of having killed a Chinese Peeping Tom. . . .

Under the status-of-forces agreements, an offense committed by United States service men against foreign nationals is within the jurisdiction of United States courts-martial if the offense arises "out of an act or omission done in the performance of official duty." Otherwise it is within the jurisdiction of the host country's courts.

However, the host country has the final decision, in case of dispute, over whether an offense is, or is not, committed in performance of duty.

Facts of the Incident

In the Girard case, the basic facts of what happened are not in dispute. The incident, as described by Secretaries Dulles and Wilson today, happened in this way:

A number of Japanese were on the firing range gathering empty brass cartridge cases. These civilians had created such a risk of injury to themselves during morning exercises that the commanding officer withdrew live ammunition before the start of the afternoon exercises.

In the interval between the two exercises, Girard and another soldier were ordered to guard a machine gun and other equipment. It was during this interval that Girard put a cartridge case in his grenade launcher, fired it, and killed Mme. Sakai.

The grenade launcher is a device that fastens on the muzzle of a rifle. The firing of a blank charge in place of a regular cartridge in the rifle launches an explosive grenade for an arched flight up to 100 yards. In this case an empty cartridge case rather than a grenade was launched.

Under the treaty provisions, the case went to the Joint United States-Japan Committee. The United States representative asked for military jurisdiction because the divisional commander had certified that Girard's action was committed in the performance of duty.

The Japanese held that it was not part of his duty to fire at the scavengers, that the firing was done between exercises, and that Girard had thrown out empty shell cases to entice the scavengers to come closer. Girard denied this, and said that he had been merely trying to frighten the scavengers.

For the first time in more than 14,000 alleged offenses against Japanese law, Japanese officials claimed their right to judge whether the offense was connected with performance of duty.

With the Joint United States-Japan Committee deadlocked, the United States representative was finally authorized on May 16 to surrender jurisdiction. There was an immediate uproar in Congress, and the next day Secretary Wilson ordered that Girard be held in United States custody pending a review.

The Wilson order brought an outcry in Japan. Since a treaty question was involved, as well as Japanese-American relations, the State Department at this point stepped into the situation, and the question was ultimately carried to the President. [The trial of Girard in a Japanese court ended in a three-year suspended sentence for Girard in late 1957—Eds.]

UNITED STATES AGREES TO WITHDRAW TROOPS FROM JAPAN [10]

The United States agreed . . . [on June 21, 1957] to a prompt withdrawal of all its ground combat forces from Japan.

In step with the buildup of Japan's own defense force, it also pledged to cut the strength of its other military elements stationed there.

This was announced in a communiqué concluding the three-day visit of Premier Nobusuke Kishi. There was no immediate Defense Department estimate of how many men would be involved in the initial cutback.

The Pentagon estimated, however, that Army and Air Force elements stationed in Japan totaled about 35,000 men. The Air Force and Army supply and administrative elements are not affected by the first-stage cutback.

The United States Government was also understood to be studying Japanese requests for assistance in various forms, totaling about $500 million.

In addition, Mr. Kishi was reported to have notified the Administration that Japan would soon follow the British lead and step up her non-strategic trade with Communist China.

The Premier was said to have been unsuccessful in his efforts to gain for Japan a voice in governing the Ryukyu and Bonin Islands, territory seized by the United States in World War II and now used for defense purposes by this country.

The communiqué supplied generalities on all points except the ground troop withdrawal agreement. . . .

[10] From "U.S. Agrees to Withdraw Combat Troops in Japan; Studies 500 Million in Aid," by Russell Baker, of the New York *Times* Washington Bureau. New York *Times*. p 1+. June 22, 1957. Reprinted by permission.

Administration officials emphasized that the decision to start a military cutback in Japan was not prompted by the controversial case of Specialist 3/c William S. Girard. In fact, it was understood that the basic decision had been taken some time ago but that the announcement was delayed to coincide with Mr. Kishi's visit.

The communiqué, nevertheless, was a far cry from the advance billing that was given the meeting by the White House, which had said no specific agreements were expected to result from the talks. Indeed, high Army officials said tonight the troop withdrawal announcement caught them completely by surprise. It had been their understanding that no reduction was planned for some time yet. . . .

The basic decision . . . was being interpreted here tonight as the start of a general United States military pullout from Japan phased to the buildup of Japanese military forces.

There are several reasons for the United States action. One primary factor from Washington's viewpoint is budgetary. Another is the fact that the large military community in Japan is an inevitable point of friction increasingly apt to touch off trouble such as the recent Taiwan (Formosa) riots and the dispute surrounding the Girard case.

The communiqué said that an intergovernmental committee would be established to study the present Security Treaty of 1951, under which the troops are kept in Japan.

The committee's functions will be to consult on the disposition and use of United States forces in Japan and to "assure that any action taken under the treaty conforms to the principles of the United Nations Charter."

JAPANESE SOCIALISTS MAP ANTI-WEST POLICY [11]

The Central Committee of the opposition Socialist party concluded a two-day session . . . [on June 28, 1957] with adoption of a foreign policy report that would, in effect, put Japan in a position of opposition to the Western world.

It also adopted a "criticism" of Premier Nobusuke Kishi's program of cooperation with the United States that denounced almost everything the Premier did in his . . . [June 1957] visit to the United States.

The eight-point program adopted as the Socialists' foreign policy if they should win power was as follows:

1. Termination of the Japanese-United States Security Treaty and immediate withdrawal of all United States military units based here.

2. Revision of the 1951 San Francisco Peace Treaty.

3. Full economic cooperation with the Soviet Union.

4. The immediate return to Japan of Okinawa and the other Ryukyu and Bonin Islands.

5. Recognition of Communist China and establishment of diplomatic relations with Peiping.

6. Early settlement of problems between Japan and South Korea and peaceful unification of Korea.

7. Close economic cooperation with Southeast Asian nations but without any financial assistance from the United States.

8. Imposition of an international ban on the testing or use of nuclear weapons and absolute prohibition of their introduction into Japan.

[11] From "Kishi's Rivals Map Anti-West Policy." New York *Times.* p3. June 29, 1957. Reprinted by permission.

ATTEMPT TO BUILD SECURITY UPON PARADOX [12]

Our military relationships with Japan are based on paradox. We imposed upon this defeated former enemy a constitution forbidding all armed forces. By law the Japanese cannot fight even a defensive war.

We also introduced democracy. This functions so well that a strong opposition prevents amendment of crippling constitutional limitations. The arrangement seemed all right in the peaceful world we dreamed of once. But it falters now.

After the Korean conflict started we saw the illogic of the situation. At our behest and quite illegally the Japanese created an armed police and, from that nucleus, what is euphemistically termed a Self-Defense Force.

This has been developing slowly—too slowly for our revised tastes. We would like it to grow into an army of 180,000 soldiers, a small navy and an aviation of thirty-three squadrons. If this happens within four years we will be lucky.

The Japanese discovered advantages to living in an American-protected incubator. It is inexpensive. Even today . . . [Japan] invests only 1.3 per cent of its gross national income in defense—compared with 9 per cent in the United States.

It insures democracy. When there is no army, or at best a weak one, there can be no revival of a dominant military class. And it is practical. The Japanese know we must protect their islands in our own strategic interest. Therefore they can invest industrial energy that might be expended on rearmament in the manufacture of export goods.

[12] From article by C. L. Sulzberger, columnist for the New York *Times*. New York *Times*. p18. October 12, 1957. Reprinted by permission.

As might be expected from all this, the result is distinct apathy on the subject of national defense. More than two years ago we decided we could no longer afford to heavily garrison Japan, that therefore we must apply shock treatment to stimulate greater local effort. This took the form of notice that we intended to reduce and eventually to withdraw our forces.

Clever diplomacy made this economizing move appear as a gesture to our political friends. Many Japanese thought, as the reduction became evident, that it resulted from . . . [the] Kishi-Eisenhower talks. Thus the Premier gained popularity; and we saved money.

But can Japan fill the vacuum now being created? The present answer is no. Its ordnance industry lags. Conventional arms manufacture remains inadequate. And there has been virtually no start toward fabricating weapons of the future.

Furthermore, because of a political situation we created, the legal structure is hopelessly inadequate. There is no security law. It is virtually impossible to prosecute leakage of military secrets. Consequently, the United States is reluctant to furnish truly modern equipment. We won't risk giving this country such devices as Nike missiles.

With its impressive industrial complex, Japan is East Asia's greatest potential military power. But, relatively, it becomes weaker every month as we withdraw. Across the water is a Sino-Soviet force of eight thousand aircraft, one hundred submarines and seventy-five combat divisions.

Our security treaty with Japan has neither time limit nor provision for abrogation. However, Tokyo is only obligated to aid us in repelling aggression against these islands. No clause covers the possibility of another Korea or a Formosan war.

The agreement allows us bases. But were we to try to operate from them in a conflict not resulting from attack on the Japanese, we might find the going difficult. A resentful population could sabotage our communications and render key points incommunicado. No matter what treaties say, we remain here today as Tokyo's military guests. The weaker our presence becomes, the more this is true.

The paradox boils down to one all-important factor. Japan's ultimate defense shelters beneath the umbrella of our strategic striking power. In East Asian terms, where is that power based? Upon Okinawa—an island whose Japanese sovereignty we figuratively acknowledge.

But our security treaty simply doesn't guarantee this country would fight beside us in any Pacific war. Therefore our generals and admirals calculate we cannot relinquish Okinawa, a quintessentially important base. The threat of riposte from there is the greatest immediate deterrent to assault on the island chain extending through Japan and Formosa from the Aleutians to the Philippines.

This will remain the case for years to come, even when missiles replace planes. Our planners insist on retaining control of Okinawa as long as we face a powerful opponent in the Orient. Right now that seems to imply "forever." But our tenure of Okinawa increasingly poisons relations with Japan, America's most influential Eastern ally.

This embarrassment is still politely avoided in diplomatic exchanges. So, for that matter is Article Nine of the Constitution forbidding Japan "the right of belligerence." We cannot afford to let this country slip from our political sphere. But we are building forces which one day must repel it. "Paradox," says the dictionary, is a "seemingly absurd though perhaps really well-founded statement."

JAPAN AND COMMUNIST CHINA [13]

What Japanese think and feel about Communist China is largely an outgrowth of their attitudes toward the country itself and the Chinese people, attitudes that long antedate the advent of the People's Republic. The Japanese know a great deal about China, which plays an important part in their lives. Ties with China go back to the very beginnings of the Japanese nation. Over many centuries China influenced profoundly the emerging Japanese civilization. It provided Japan with its written script and with some of its ethical foundation stones in Buddhism and Confucianism. It gave the model for the traditional educational system and the very forms in which for centuries Japanese history was written. All educated Japanese are well aware of these historic ties.

When educated Japanese and Chinese meet there exists a common cultural bond. They understand the same etiquette and have read the same classical literature. Before dinner they can discuss poetry and painting, after dinner they can play Chinese chess. They can fall back on a common written script if there is any difficulty of oral understanding. The cultural bonds which link America with England are hardly closer than those which draw the two Asian neighbors together.

During the past fifty years Japan has been deeply involved in China—in wars against it or on its soil, in control of Chinese territories and people (Manchuria and Formosa), and in very close economic and cultural relations. Hundreds of thousands of Japanese have lived and worked in China, and scores of thousands of Chinese have come to Japan to secure a modern education. Mil-

[13] From chapter entitled "Japan and the Rise of Communist China," by C. Martin Wilbur, director, East Asian Institute, Columbia University, in *Japan Between East and West*. Published for the Council on Foreign Relations by Harper & Brothers. New York. 1957. p223-31. Reprinted by permission.

lions of Japanese young men served in the Army in China between 1931 and 1945. Japan is full of "China experts" and "old China hands."

Popular Attitudes Toward Communist China

It is not easy for an outsider to perceive, let alone describe, the attitudes of one people toward another. Without attempting so subtle an exercise, I should like merely to suggest a few elements that enter into the prevalent Japanese viewpoints on Communist China. One is the feeling of close relationship, mentioned above, which derives both from ancient cultural bonds and from pre-1945 economic and personal ties. This makes the present isolation from the mainland seem unnatural and uncomfortable. It accounts in part for the lively interest in all kinds of news of recent developments in China. It may also account for a sense of gratification at China's successes against the United States and at its evident internal achievements.

In addition to the feeling of cultural indebtedness, Japanese also seem to have a strong feeling of superiority toward the Chinese. Perhaps this arises in part from Japan's success in modernization while China lagged so far behind. In Japanese accounts of the material progress in China since 1949 there is a strong undertone of astonishment. Japanese seem quite confident of their ability to understand the Chinese and to handle them. Among some Japanese there are also evident feelings of remorse and guilt at the way Japan mistreated China in the past, and this in turn leads to the view that Japanese have no grounds to criticize China for the course it is following under communism. Statements by Chinese leaders exonerating the Japanese people from blame or disclaiming any desire for revenge seem to make a deep impression.

Japanese draw a clear line of distinction, whether justified or not, between Communist China and Soviet Russia. From reading the Japanese press, talking with Japanese friends about the Communist problem, or studying public opinion polls, one quickly observes that the Japanese view Russia with a great deal of suspicion and dislike. In part this is a legacy of more than a half century of contest for influence in Manchuria and Korea and for possession of Sakhalin and the Kuriles. In part it is a reaction to Russia's having broken the nonaggression treaty of 1941 and plunged into the Pacific war at the very moment when Japan was already suing for peace. It is fanned by the belief that Russia held many thousands of Japanese war prisoners for more than a decade after their surrender and allowed the death by disease and starvation of many thousands more.

Dislike of Russia does not seriously reduce the traditional affection for China merely because China has adopted the Russian path toward socialism. There is a strong belief that the Chinese revolution has been far more humane than the Russian one. Many Japanese who detest communism see no reason to fear Communist China. Or, on the contrary, a Japanese may say, "There is nothing wrong with communism, except that it was first taken up by the Slavs, who are cold-blooded." . . .

It should be emphasized that there are great differences of emphasis within the left and liberal side of the political spectrum. Communists are implacably anti-American and unqualifiedly pro-Soviet. They stand at the forefront, or just behind the scenes, of drives against rearmament and against American bases. Right-wing Socialists are more neutralist, more skeptical of the intentions of Soviet Russia and China, and cautiously in favor of a strictly controlled rearmament. Russia's brutal intervention in Hungary shocked Japanese opinion, and

Communist China's support of that action was not approved. The Socialists were split right and left, as to
where to place the blame for the Hungarian uprising
and its suppression. Many liberals are fond of America
but believe its policies toward Japan since the cold war
became intense have been misguided. On all these issues
there are many gradations of opinion.

The Political Parties and Communist China

Since 1953 the China problem has been of increasing
importance in Japanese politics, especially the question
of encouraging trade with China.

The platforms of the two major parties show clear
differences on relations with America and Communist
China. The conservative Liberal-Democratic party,
which controls about two thirds of the lower house, advocates "cooperation with free, democratic countries as
the keynote of diplomacy." It proposes to "promote reduction in the joint cost of defense, decrease in the number of military bases, and amendment of the Japan-
United States Security Treaty and the Administrative
Agreement." Referring to China and Russia, it promises
to "try to normalize or adjust diplomatic relations with
the countries with which such relations have not been
resumed." It will "pursue economic diplomacy, and try
to expand trade with various countries, especially economic cooperation with Southeast Asia and the promotion of trade with Communist China. . . ."

These rather ambiguous statements of general aims
are accompanied by policies of promoting close cooperation with the United States in trade and rearmament,
participation in the embargo against the sale of strategic
goods to Communist China, and the absence of any obvious effort to enter into diplomatic relations with

Peking. However, both Yoshida and Hatoyama, and more recently Ishibashi and Kishi, have found the pressure of public opinion and of some business groups running so strongly in favor of facilitating trade with China that the government has taken some steps in that direction. The party's platform accepts this as necessary. Furthermore, the government is moving toward forms of quasi-recognition. . . . [It has been] reported that a postal agreement is likely to be concluded for the exchange of postal matter between China and Japan, although the Foreign Office has pointed out that this step has nothing to do with the question of recognition. . . .

The Social-Democratic party caps its views toward the United States and Communist China by a broader theory—that Japan and China working together should attempt to form a bridge between America and Russia in the Far East. To bring this about Japan should persuade the United States to give up the Mutual Security Treaty of September 1951, and China should persuade Russia to give up the Sino-Soviet Treaty of February 1950, which unites those countries against the possibility of attack by Japan or a country allied to it. Then the security of both China and Japan should be guaranteed by a multilateral collective security pact among the four countries.

In sum, all Japanese political parties favor trade and diplomatic relations with Communist China. They disagree only on the manner and timing. To the Communists and the left wing of the Social-Democratic party, close relations with China are a point of cardinal importance. They want full relations established immediately. Members of the right wing in the Socialist party are troubled about the problem of Formosa and do not wish to imperil good relations with the United States through a precipitate move to open relations with China. Leaders of the conservative party also favor trade and other relations but feel under heavy pressure from the American government to delay and proceed cautiously. They have held back, at some risk to their own political positions, against the strong tide within Japanese public opinion.

OUTLOOK FOR THE FUTURE [14]

Japan is the only thoroughly modernized nation in Asia, the only major center of industrial power, and the only Asian country that has ranked as a first-rate military power in modern times. Yet the free world has made nothing of this great potential in its struggle against totalitarianism. We have been content to keep Japan a minor American problem rather than to help her become a major asset for the democratic side.

If Japan does not become a major asset for our side, there is always the possibility—it is fortunately not a probability at the present time—that she might join the Communist camp. As a working member of the opposition, she could easily restore herself as the greatest military force in all Asia. Her industrial strength and technical skills would unquestionably insure the success of the Chinese Communists. Such a defection, in fact, might well prove the death blow to democratic hopes in Asia.

What, in contrast to this possibility, has the free world done to develop the Japanese potential? Very little. Nothing significant has been attempted and, worse still, neither the partisans of democracy in Japan nor the leaders of the Western democracies even visualize Japan in these terms.

[14] From "To Make Japan an Asset to Democracy," article by Edwin O. Reischauer, professor of Far Eastern languages, Harvard University, and author of *Wanted: An Asian Policy*. New York *Times Magazine*. p23. August 26, 1956. Reprinted by permission.

Japan's possible contribution to the democracies falls roughly into three categories—military, economic and ideological. And the most vital of these is the ideological. It is clear that the military role of a democratic Japan cannot in the foreseeable future be more than that of a useful base for the free world—and even then useful only in a limited war. Her economic potential could indeed be as valuable to the democratic world as to the Communists, not only in terms of goods and machines (Japan represents the greatest concentration of factory power in all Asia), but also through full use of her vast technical knowledge. But it is in the third category that Japan presents the potential of greatest value; her success as a working democracy may prove to be a psychological factor of the greatest importance in the battle for Asia.

A Demonstration of Democracy in Asia

It is no small thing that Asia's most advanced nation is a living demonstration that democracy can work successfully in an Asian cultural setting and at Asian economic levels. The successes of this experiment in democracy speak for themselves. The failures—and they have been many and serious—would prove instructive as a working plan of the pitfalls that threaten the newer Asian democracies.

Many Asians, mostly notably the Chinese, have already abandoned their earlier hope that democracy is a realistic pattern of social and political organization. The problem, therefore, is not to convince them that ideal democracy is a beautiful theory or even to demonstrate to them that it has proved a marvelously successful mechanism in some parts of the Western world. The real problem is to convince them that it is a practical pattern for Asians and then to help them prove the truth of this bold hypothesis in the face of the obvious difficulties. Here the Japanese could help. Their experts in sociological and political problems would probably be of more value in Asian countries than would Western experts in the same field, simply because the personal experience of the Japanese—economically and culturally —has always been closer to that of other Asian nations than has our own.

We are not the only ones who have overlooked Japan's various potentialities in the battle for Asia. The Japanese themselves, as well as the other peoples of Asia, have been equally blind. The Japanese still have not recovered their self-confidence after their catastrophic attempt to carve out an empire and they are content to leave to us the worries of solving the world's problems.

Asian Attitudes Toward Japan

The blindness of the other peoples of Asia is still easier to explain. Those closest to Japan fear the Japanese for their past aggressions, hate them for the destruction and suffering their armies brought and despise them for having failed in their foolhardy attempt to conquer the Far East. Such antipathies become progressively weaker the further west one goes in Asia, but they are replaced not by respect for Japan but by complete indifference. All Asians, despite their emotional pan-Asian bias, in reality continue to look toward the West and to ignore with some disdain the rest of their own continent. And Japan in particular is ignored by the other Asian nations because its relationship with the United States is commonly considered to be semi-colonial. . . .

While it is primarily up to the Japanese to determine their own role in Asia, the United States can at least be of assistance in bringing Japan and the rest of Asia into more beneficial contact with each other. Asian suspicion and resentment of the United States unquestionably limit our role as a sponsor in Asian society of an equally unpopular Japan, but much can still be accomplished if we are willing to exercise tact and imagination. We could help the Japanese solve the disputes over reparations that stand between them and some other Asian peoples; we could do more than we are doing to use Japanese technical skills and industrial power in the economic aid programs we are sponsoring in Asia; we could certainly help the Japanese realize the full economic potentiality of which they are capable.

More important than such specific steps, however, would be a basic change in attitude. We have concentrated on Japan's very limited role as a military base and thereby have allowed her more significant potential to go begging. For just as a Japanese switch to communism would probably prove the decisive factor in a Communist triumph throughout Asia, Japan's continued success with the democratic pattern of life might well prove the most important psychological factor in the eventual victory of democracy in that vast area.

BIBLIOGRAPHY

An asterisk (*) preceding a reference indicates that the article or a part of it has been reprinted in this book.

BOOKS AND PAMPHLETS

Benedict, Ruth. Chrysanthemum and the sword. 324p. Houghton Mifflin Co. Boston. '46.

Bisson, T. A. Prospects for democracy in Japan. 143p. Institute of Pacific Relations. 1 E. 54th St. New York 22. '49.

Borton, Hugh, ed. Japan. 320p. Oxford University Press. New York. '52.

Borton, Hugh. Japan's modern century. 524p. Ronald Press Co. New York. '55.

Bronfenbrenner, M. Prospects of Japanese democracy. (Behind the Headlines. v 15, no3) 17p. Institute of Pacific Relations. 1 E. 54th St. New York 22. '55.

Cohen, J. B. Japan's economy in war and reconstruction. 545p. Institute of Pacific Relations. New York. '49.

*Consulate General of Japan. Foreign minister outlines principles of Japan's foreign policy. Aiichiro Fujiyama. (Japan Report. v3, no 15) 4p. The Consulate. 3 E. 54th St. New York 22. '57.

Consulate General of Japan. Japan today. 27p. The Consulate. 3 E. 54th St. New York 22. '57.

Consulate General of Japan. Japan's constitutional problems and her political chart. Tosiyosi Miyasawa. (Japan's Problems Series) 9p. The Consulate. 3 E. 54th St. New York 22. '56.

Consulate General of Japan. Japan's foreign trade. Ryokichi Minobe. (Japan's Problems Series) 19p. The Consulate. 3 E. 54th St. New York 22. '56.

Consulate General of Japan. Japan's international cultural activities. 48p. The Consulate. 3 E. 54th St. New York 22. '55.

Consulate General of Japan. Japan's labor problems. Ichiro Nakayama. (Japan's Problems Series) 17p. The Consulate. 3 E. 54th St. New York 22. '56.

Consulate General of Japan. Major foreign policy speeches. Mamoru Shigemitsu. 24p. The Consulate. 3 E. 54th St. New York 22. '55.

Consulate General of Japan. Prime Minister Kishi visits the United States, June, 1957. 16p. The Consulate. 3 E. 54th St. New York 22. '57.

Consulate General of Japan. Rehabilitation of Japan's economy and Asia. Saburo Okita. (Japan's Problems Series) 16p. The Consulate. 3 E. 54th St. New York 22. '56.

Consulate General of Japan. Review of Japan's defense strength. Keikichi Masuhara. (Japan's Problems Series) 22p. The Consulate. 3 E. 54th St. New York 22. '56.

*Council on Foreign Relations. Japan between East and West. 327p. Harper & Bros. New York. '57.
    Reprinted in this book: Japan and the rise of Communist China. C. M. Wilbur. p223-31.

Elling, P. W. Japan. 40p. Japan Society. c/o Savoy-Plaza Hotel. Fifth Ave. at 58th St. New York 22.

Fisher, Harold. Japanese attitudes toward American policy. (Journeys Behind the News v 17, no 12). 5p. Social Science Foundation. c/o University of Denver. Denver 10, Colo. '54.

Hersey, John. Hiroshima. 117p. Alfred A. Knopf. New York. '46.

Ike, Nobutaka. Japanese politics. 300p. Alfred A. Knopf. New York. '57.

*Japan. Ministry of Foreign Affairs. Public Information and Cultural Affairs Bureau. Japan as it is today. 87p. The Bureau. Tokyo. '56.
    Obtainable from Consulate General of Japan. 3 E. 54th St. New York 22.

Kublin, Hyman. What shall I read on Japan. 16p. 4th ed. rev. Japan Society. 18 E. 50th St. New York 22. '57.
    Bibliography.

Latourette, K. S. History of Japan. rev. ed. 299p. Macmillan Co. New York. '57.

Linebarger, P. M. A. and others. Far Eastern governments and politics, China and Japan. 2d ed. 643p. D. Van Nostrand Co. Princeton, N.J. '56.

Nagai, Takashi. We of Nagasaki; tr. by Ichiro Shirato and H. B. L. Silverman. 189p. Duell, Sloan & Pearce. New York. '51.

Newsweek Club and Educational Bureaus. Japan: a free world dilemma. 22p. The Bureaus. 152 W. 42d St. New York 18. '54.

Quigley, H. S. and Turner, J. E. New Japan: government and politics. 456p. University of Minnesota Press. Minneapolis. '56.

Reischauer, E. O. Japan, past and present. 2d ed. 292p. Alfred A. Knopf. New York. '52.

Reischauer, E. O. United States and Japan. rev. ed. 394p. Harvard University Press. Cambridge, Mass. '57.

Reischauer, E. O. Wanted: an Asian policy. 276p. Alfred A. Knopf. New York. '55.

Sansom, G. B. Japan in world history. 95p. Institute of Pacific Relations. 1 E. 54th St. New York 22. '51.

Swearingen, Rodger and Langer, P. F. Red flag in Japan. 276p. Harvard University Press. Cambridge, Mass. '52.

Tiedemann, A. E. Modern Japan. (Anvil original no9) 192p. D. Van
Nostrand Co. Princeton, N.J. '55.
Vining, E. G. Windows for the crown prince. 320p. J. B. Lippincott
Co. Philadelphia. '52.
*Webb, Herschel. Introduction to Japan. 2d ed. 145p. Columbia
University Press. New York. '57.
Yanago, Chitoshi. Japanese people and politics. 408p. John Wiley &
Sons. New York. '56.

PERIODICALS

Academy of Political Science. Proceedings. 26:71-115. Ja. '55. Eco-
nomic and political position of Japan.
America. 89:213-15. My. 23, '53. Roots of Japanese anti-American-
ism. R. L. G. Deverall.
America. 97:379-80. Jl. 6, '57. Mr. Kishi's new era.
America. 98:310-12. D. 7, '57. Hope for Japan, 1958. Colin Clark.
American Historical Review. 60:818-29. Jl. '55. Japanese nationalism
and expansionism. Hilary Conroy.
American Political Science Review. 50:980-1010. D. '56. Origins of
the present Japanese constitution. R. E. Ward.
American Quarterly. 7:247-56. Fall '55. Young Japan's anti-Ameri-
canism. Hilary Conroy.
American Scholar. 24:443-55. Fall '55. What the Japanese intellec-
tuals are thinking. Dallas Finn.
Annals of the American Academy of Political and Social Science.
294:1-243. Jl. '54. America and a new Asia. J. C. Charlesworth,
ed.
Annals of the American Academy of Political and Social Science.
305:101-13. My. '56. Approaches of the Japanese innovator to
cultural and technical change. J. W. Bennett; R. K. McKnight.
*Annals of the American Academy of Political and Social Science.
308:1-236. N. '56. Japan since recovery of independence. K. E.
Colton and others, eds.
    Reprinted in this book: Japanese communism and the Moscow-Peking
axis. Rodger Swearingen. p63-75.
Atlantic Monthly. 194:30-5. N. '54. Japan at the crossroads. A. H.
Dean.
*Atlantic Monthly. 195:97-174. Ja. '55. Perspective of Japan; an
Atlantic supplement assembled by Intercultural Publications Inc.
    Reprinted in this book: Popular entertainments of Japan. Koji Ozaki
(tr. by Donald Keene). p148-51; Japan's "cultural democracy." Nyozekan
Hasegawa (tr. by William Candlewood). p170-3; Chronology of Japanese
history. p174.
    Also separate: 78p. Intercultural Publications Inc. 60 E. 42d St. New
York 22. '55.
*Atlantic Monthly. 198:17-22. Ag. '56. Atlantic report on the world
today—Japan.

Atlantic Monthly. 198:55-7. Ag. '56. Southern cotton and Japan.
D. L. Cohn.
Reply. 198:32+. D. '56. J. L. Severance.
Atlantic Monthly. 199:20+. Mr. '57. Atlantic report—Japan.
Atlantic Monthly. 200:19-23. O. '57. Atlantic report—Japan.
*Bulletin of the Atomic Scientists. 11:289-92. O. '55. Japan and the
H-Bomb. Herbert Passin.
*Business Week. p 148+. S. 24, '55. Made-in-Japan: a new record.
Business Week. p 126+. Je. 22, '57. Japan's bid to regain its place
in the sun.
Business Week. p 102. Ag. 3, '57. Japan nears its export goal.
Business Week. p 154+. S. 7, '57. Japan upgrades its old label.
Catholic World. 182:364-70. F. '56. How red the Rising Sun? P. K.
Brooks.
Christian Century. 74:983-5. Ag. 21, '57. Japan walks a tightrope;
Christian Century world seminar. H. E. Fey.
Christian Century. 74:1208. O. 9, '57. Bomb protest aftermath.
W. P. Woodard.
*Collier's. 137:58-67. Mr. 2, '56. Japan. Peter Kalischer.
Commentary. 23:466-70. My. '57. Japan's lost generation. Peter
Schmid.
Contemporary Review. 192:37-41. Jl. '57. Japan today. W. J. Moore.
Current History. 31:15-19. Jl. '56. Japan: ally for peace. H. S.
Quigley.
Current History. 33:353-7. D. '57. Chinese-Japanese courtship. H. S.
Quigley.
Economist. 180:571-2+. Ag. 18, '56. Arms and Japan.
Economist. 180:641-2. Ag. 25, '56. Orphan of Asia.
Economist. 180:868-9. S. 15, '56. Japanese table-turning.
Economist. 182:891-2. Mr. 16, '57. Peaceful co-prosperity?
Economist. 183:603-4. My. 18, '57. Mr. Kishi in search of face.
Far Eastern Quarterly. 14:355-63. My. '55. Old values and new
techniques in the modernization of Japan. T. C. Smith.
Far Eastern Quarterly. 15:57-75. N. '55. Management and industrial
relations in postwar Japan. S. B. Levine.
Far Eastern Survey. 24:71-5. My. '55. Prime minister's office and
executive power in Japan. J. M. Maki.
Far Eastern Survey. 25:49-58. Ap. '56. Constitution and the current
Japanese politics. R. E. Ward.
*Far Eastern Survey. 25:168-74. N. '56. Japan between two worlds.
H. S. Quigley.
Far Eastern Survey. 26:129-40. S. '57. Japanese exports and the
American market. W. S. Hunsberger.
Foreign Affairs. 33:402-15. Ap. '55. Japan reconsiders. Lily Abegg.
Foreign Affairs. 34:40-9. O. '55. Japan's new role in east Asia.
Toshikazu Kase.

Foreign Affairs. 34:227-44. Ja. '56. Japan at cross-purposes. H. F. Armstrong.

Foreign Affairs. 34:459-68. Ap. '56. False assumptions about the Japanese economy. Nobutane Kiuchi.

*Foreign Policy Bulletin. 36:172+. Ag. 1, '57. Japan's year of decisions. V. M. Dean.

Foreign Policy Bulletin. 36:183-4. Ag. 15, '57. Japan and Far East security. V. M. Dean.

Fortune. 56:106-13+. Jl. '57. In Japan it's Jimmu keiki. John Davenport.

Fortune. 56:96+. O. '57. Japan holds the line.

Harper's Magazine. 215:27-36. D. '57; 216:48-55. Ja.; 72-9. F. '58. Voyage of the Lucky Dragon. R. E. Lapp.

International Affairs. 31:291-9. Jl. '55. Present economic situation in Japan. G. C. Allen.

Journal of Economic History. 16:165-81. Je. '56. Landlords and rural capitalists in the modernization of Japan. T. C. Smith.

Journal of Modern History. 29:108-11. Je. '57. Roots of Japanese imperialism: a memorandum of General LeGendre [with text]. E. L. Presseisen.

Nation. 178:333-4. Ap. 17, '54. Japan revisited. W. M. Ball.

Nation's Business. 43:70-81. Ap. 55. Keep out! Japan tells U. S. investors. Richard Tregaskis.

New Leader. 40:12-14. O. 14, '57. Why Japan is only half-modern: the occidental apparatus and the old moral structure. Takeo Naoi.

New Republic. 128:12-14. Jl. 20, '53. Batto-tai is sung again. H. H. Tiltman.

New Republic. 132:3-4. My. 9, '55. Resistance in Japan.

New Republic. 132:9-11. My. 30, '55. Trade with red China. H. H. Tiltman.

New Republic. 136:10-12. Ap. 22, '57. Japan and China. S. C. Leng.

*New York Times. p 1+. Mr. 11, '56. Bonin Isles' 178 residents seen as pawns in power game. Robert Trumbull.

*New York Times. p 12. Ap. 12, '56. Boycott of Japan upsets officials. Elie Abel.

New York Times. p 17. Ap. 18, '56. Ryukyuans look to Japanese ties. Robert Trumbull.

*New York Times. p47+. Ja. 3, '57. Japan regains place as industrial great. Robert Trumbull.

*New York Times. p 1+. Je. 5, '57. U.S. agrees to let Japanese try G.I. in woman's death. E. W. Kenworthy.

*New York Times. p 1+. Je. 22, '57. U.S. agrees to withdraw combat troops in Japan; studies 500 million in aid. Russell Baker.

*New York Times. p3. Je. 29, '57. Kishi's rivals map anti-west policy.

*New York Times. p3. Jl. 17, '57. Japan joins race for China trade. Foster Hailey.

*New York Times. p 18. O. 12, '57. Attempt to build security upon paradox. C. L. Sulzberger.

*New York Times. p26. O. 14, '57. Can Asian flu come to America? C. L. Sulzberger.

New York Times. p 1+. Ja. 13, '58. Pro-red is victor in Okinawa vote. Robert Trumbull.

New York Times. p 1+. Ja. 22, '58. U.S. land reform law in Japan foils red drive to win farmer. Robert Trumbull.

*New York Times Magazine. p12+. S. 6, '53. Yoshida—'deep bows and a temper.' Lindesay Parrott.

*New York Times Magazine. p23. Ag. 26, '56. To make Japan an asset to democracy. E. O. Reischauer.

*New York Times Magazine. p29+. Ap. 7, '57. Okinawa: a 'sometimes painful' lesson for us. Robert Trumbull.

New Yorker. 33:33-4+. Je. 22, '57. Letter from Tokyo. Anthony West.

New Yorker. 33:57-90. D. 7, '57. Our far-flung correspondents—game on a hill [the Girard case]. John Hersey.

*Newsweek. 43:60-1. Ap. 12, '54. Comeback of the great Japan trade combines.

Newsweek. 49:49-51. Je. 24, '57. Helmsman and Japan today.

Newsweek. 50:16-17. Jl. 1, '57. What Kishi wanted.

*Political Quarterly. 27:141-51. Ap. '56. Ultranationalism in postwar Japan. M. B. Jansen.

*Political Science Quarterly. 70:410-20. S. '55. Past limitations and the future of democracy in Japan. Hugh Borton.

Reporter. 10:30-5. F. 16, '54. Anti-Americanism in Japan; ed. by C. H. Kawakami.

*Reporter. 14:23-6. Mr. 8, '56. Between Marx and the Middle Ages. Lily Abegg.

*Saturday Evening Post. 225:24-5+. Ap. 4, '53. Japs have us on the griddle now. Demaree Bess.

Saturday Evening Post. 230:18-19+. Ag. 10, '57. Are we driving Japan into red China's arms? Cameron Hawley.

Senior Scholastic. 69:8-10+. O. 4, '56. Japan, problem child of the Far East.

*Time. 65:34-7. Mr. 14, '55. Japan—land of the reluctant sparrows.

Time. 69:24+. Je. 3, '57. Co-prosperity again.

Time. 70:17. Jl. 1, '57. Kudos for Kishi.

Time. 70:106+. N. 18, '57. Naka-darumi in Japan .

United Nations World. 7:27-30+. Ap. '53. Japan, America's schizoid ally. H. H. Smythe.

United Nations World. 7:38-42. S. '53. Will Japan bow to the East? H. H. Smythe.

*United States Department of State Bulletin. 30:971-3. Je. 28, '54. Security in the Pacific; speech made before the Los Angeles World Affairs Council, June 11, 1954. J. F. Dulles.

United States Department of State Bulletin. 32:1051-5. Je. 27, '55. Agreement reached on Japan's participation in GATT.

United States Department of State Bulletin. 34:974-7. Je. 11, '56. U.S. Trade mission to Japan.

United States Department of State Bulletin. 37:534-5. S. 30, '57. Relationship between U.S.-Japanese security treaty and U.N. charter.

*Virginia Quarterly Review. 31:383-400. Summer '55. United States and Japan: a new century begins. Ralph Braibanti.

Virginia Quarterly Review. 33:17-27. Winter '57. How new is the new Japan? H. S. Quigley.

Vital Speeches of the Day. 21:879-80. D. 1, '54. Japan and southeast Asia; address, November 8, 1954. Shigeru Yoshida.

Western Political Quarterly. 8:545-68. D. '55. Japan's rearmament: progress and problems. J. M. Maki.

Western Political Quarterly. 10:457-9. Je. '57. Prognosis on Japan. D. H. Mendel, Jr.

Woman's Home Companion. 82:9+. Je. '55. Japan, a yen with two sides. H. Holly.

World Politics. 8:423-32. Ap. '56. Problems of democratic adjustment in modern Japan. R. E. Ward.

World Politics. 9:37-54. O. '56. Japan's response to the West; the contrast with China. W. W. Lockwood.

World Today. 11:6-8. Ja. '55. Japan after the fall of Mr. Yoshida.

World Today. 11:458-60. N. '55. Socialist merger and the balance of parties in Japan.

Yale Review. 46:571-85. Summer '57. Japanese politics and the Socialist minority. Hyman Kublin.

Yale Review. 47:198-218. Winter '58. Japan's foreign policy. Yasushi Akashi.